More Than a
Garage Band

To KG
Forever
TK
"Crazy"

More Than a Garage Band

A Journey of Celebration, Crisis, and Connection

By Tom Kemper

Artwork by Louis Carosello,
see story, page 211

Copyright © 2018 by Tom Kemper
All rights reserved

ISBN 978-0-9973601-2-7

Printed in the United States

Dedicated to my late brother Tim (capitol T-I-M) Kemper, and my grandson, James Kemper.

𝄞

IN MEMORIUM

Chuck Berry
Father of Rock n Roll, died March 18, 2017,
and
Gregg Allman
a founding member of *The Allman Brothers*,
died May 27, 2017, who passed during
the writing of this book.

Acknowledgements

Editor	Barbara Harris
Book cover design	David Kemper, *Cloud Craft Studios*
Book cover assistance	Louis Carosello
Front cover photo	Janie Kemper
Back cover drawing (1973)	Peter Sullivan
Title page design	Louis Carosello
Book title creator	Terry Martin
Prologue writer	Michael "Supe" Granda, *Ozark Mountain Daredevils*
Proof reader	Christi Kemper
Book designer and typesetter	Kristie Lee

Most of all, I'd like to thank Bob Schnieders, Terry Martin, Bob Lawder, and Billy Bicklehaupt for putting up with me during the writing of this adventure. I know at times you guys wondered about what the heck I was doing. In the end, I hope I served you well...and to my editor, Barb Harris who not only edited this book, but also took the time to teach me how to write. Without her help, this book would have not seen the light of day.

Contents

Illustrations xi

Prologue: Courtesy of Michael "Supe" Granda
of *The Ozark Mountain Daredevils* xiii

Introduction 1

Chapter 1. Baseball, Bubble Gum, and Rock n Roll 3

Chapter 2. Long Haired Music............................. 8

Chapter 3. The Volcano and Boats Birthday Party 25

Chapter 4. It 45

Chapter 5. Invasion 55

Chapter 6. God's Gifted 71

Chapter 7. Black Sheep Bird................................ 88

Chapter 8. *Daredevils* and *The King* 102

Chapter 9. No Bummer Summer?........................ 120

Chapter 10. Tick, Tick, Tick............................... 135

Chapter 11. Moving on and Out 156

Chapter 12. *Del Alma*.................................... 174

Chapter 13. End of the Rainbow 196

A Bible For Bands: The Rules for
Becoming a Professional Band........................ 219

Illustrations

Figure 1. Craze's House 1
Figure 2. The steps across the street 2
Figure 3. Craze at age 13 9
Figure 4. *The Vegas* with Steve, Peter, Craze, and Dennis 20
Figure 5. *The Vegas* with Peter, Lawder, Skinner, and Craze .. 36
Figure 6. Boat's house 41
Figure 7. Webster Groves YMCA 44
Figure 8. The church 48
Figure 9. Castaway's business card 72
Figure 10. The *Admiral*, Arch, and Old Courthouse 114
Figure 11. "Blue Salon" ballroom on the *Admiral* 115
Figure 12. *Jefferson Airplane* poster 119
Figure 13. *Grateful Dead* and *Public Service* flyer 129
Figure 14. *Canned Heat* and *Public Service* flyer 131
Figure 15. Pictures of Gerry Garcia 134
Figure 16. *Boogie Band* business card 148
Figure 17. "VP" Ball, *Albert King* and *Sound Farm* 157
Figure 18. The sons and grandson 217
Figure 19. Peter, Eyes's, Lawder, Craze,
Billy, Strings, and Bird 218

Prologue

Courtesy of Michael "Supe" Granda,
Ozark Mountain Daredevils

The 60's were exciting, though tumultuous, times.

Everyone remembers exactly where he or she was on November 22, 1963, when they learned of John F. Kennedy's assassination.

Everyone remembers exactly where he or she was on July 20, 1969, when man stepped onto the moon for the first time.

Everyone remembers exactly where they were on February 9, 1964, when John, Paul, George, and Ringo stepped onto the stage of the Ed Sullivan Theater for the first time, slinging everyone deep into the throes of *Beatlemania*.

I remember exactly where I was on that winter, Sunday night —smack dab in front of my family's black and white *Motorola* console television in south St. Louis County. That slack-jaw moment would shape the rest of my life. The very next day, I rushed out to *Mel Bay Music*, got a guitar, found some guys and formed a band of my own.

It was also the day when youngsters all over St. Louis abandoned their dream of playing for the *Cardinals*, replacing it with a dream of playing in a rock-n-roll band. As icing on the cake, the girls weren't screaming for baseball players.

Five others, who were also smack dab in front of their family televisions, were Craze, Strings, Peter, Lawder and Eyes, who also formed a band of their own—*The Public Service*.

While the four lads from Liverpool were stepping onto the world stage, these five lads from St. Louis would begin stepping onto stages all around the Gateway City.

While my band, *The Coachmen Four*, wouldn't make much of a ripple on the local music scene, Craze, Strings, Peter, Lawder and Eyes would. In the latter part of the 60's ('65-'69 to be exact), *The Public Service* would make quite a splash around town.

They were much better musicians, while also more confidant and entertaining, than most of the other outfits around town. In a word, they were downright GOOD.

Peter and I were classmates at *Lindbergh High School*. While the rest of our peers were still infatuated with snazzy cars, greasy hair, cigarettes, cheerleaders and beer, Peter and I found ourselves immersed in this new world of rock-n-roll. We would often sit in our classroom and talk about guitars and music and gigs —oh, my.

The local, St. Louis music scene of the 60's was a rich palette of swinging rhythm-n-blues and funky rock-n-roll. Hell, *Chuck Berry* lived there until the day he died. The parties he threw out on his farm in Wentzville are still legendary.

Often, you could catch sets around town by *Ike & Tina Turner*, as well as *The Isley Brothers*, *Oliver Sain*, and *Bob Kuban* (all residents of the area). The city was—and still is—a hotbed of rockin' rock-n-roll.

I became an absolute, musical sponge. I could not cram enough music into my teen-age noggin. When I wasn't playing music, I was thinking about playing music. When I wasn't thinking about playing music, I was in search of others, who were thinking about and playing music.

Often times, this path led me to *The Public Service*. When they played, I loved tagging along. I could be found just hanging around, digging the music coming from the stage (as well as the scene unfolding around it).

Their musicianship was top notch.

Their repertoire was excellent.

Their personalities were exuberant and fun.

Their camaraderie and teamwork was contagious.

I, vividly, remember catching them, as they warmed up for the *Grateful Dead* at the *St. Louis Armory*, the *Jefferson Airplane* at *Kiel Auditorium*, and the *Allman Joy* (forerunner to the *Allman Bros.*) at the *Castaways Club* and the *Rainy Days*.

Their show-stopping versions of *The Music Machine's*, "Talk, Talk" and *The Who's*, "My Generation" were just that—show-stopping.

When they finished their gigs, I enjoyed helping them haul their gear off the stage and into their van. To this day, I still enjoy this part of the whole process.

Garages all across the land filled with rock-n-roll bands of all shapes and sizes. Fathers' cars and lawn mowers were rolled out into the driveway to make room for amplifiers and drums. Many evenings, my father's car found its way out into our driveway, so *The Coachmen Four* could find their way through "Louie, Louie" and "In the Midnight Hour".

The Public Service found their way into numerous garages, as they found their way onto St. Louis stages and into the hearts of their many fans.

Time, though, would take its toll. High school days ended, colleges called and life's funny way of unfolding, unfolded. All of these gentlemen would move on to other walks of life—every one of them, successful.

Though, they may have vanished from the spotlight, for those of us who followed them, they will live forever in our foggy memories.

They were one of the first to coin - and help define the phrase, 'garage band'.

But, folks, this was more than a garage band.

More Than a Garage Band

Introduction

This mid-sixties story begins among the large trees and one-hundred-year-old homes in the middle-class town of Webster Groves, a suburb of Saint Louis, Missouri. Four thirteen-year-old boys discover rock music, join forces, and undertake their own unique adventure of companionship, fun, and disillusionment on their quest for stardom in the world of *garage bands*.

Figure 1. Craze's House.

Figure 2. The steps across the street.

Chapter 1

Baseball, Bubble Gum, and Rock n Roll

Craze stared down at the pile of thin-cut, pink rectangles. "Put three of these babies in your mouth and you got somethin'," referring to the sticks of gum that came in the packs of baseball cards he had just purchased.

"I paid a nickel for each pack and they're worth every penny… and you get a piece of gum to boot…what a deal."

He inspected the first piece and bit in. It shattered in his mouth like a plate-glass window. Most of the time, the gum dried out in the pack and almost broke his teeth. But with a little work, two or three pieces made for a great wad of sweetness.

"Darn, this piece is gonna be tough," he thought. "Getting this gum ready takes a lot of work and spit. But I'm not about to waste a perfectly good piece of gum just because it got a little hard in the pack."

He sloshed the gum around in his mouth. "Just right."

Craze carefully removed the wad from his mouth and set it on the curb next to his baseball cards.

"Okay, here we go again," he said as he repeated the process all over again. "Pick the right piece, shove in mouth, and chew."

The second piece assumed its position next to the first piece on the curb.

"A third and final piece…" he thought as his jaws began to hurt.

"Now, pick up the first two pieces and shove 'em in my mouth."

At last came the reward, three sweet, soft, and juicy pieces of gum. Finally ready, Craze announced out loud: "PLAY BALL!"

The juice ran out of the side of his mouth and down his cheek, and Craze faced his next problem. "Somehow I gotta lick my fingers so the ball don't get sticky."

At twelve years old, Craze dreamed of a career in the big leagues. With over one hundred kids living on the block, Craze usually had several kids to pick from for a game of baseball. His mother once said, "I counted one hundred twenty six kids living on this street."

The location of the game might be in the street, or in one of the kids' back yards or—even better—on the school playground one block away. But, on this day, with no other kids available, Craze looked at this dilemma as an opportunity, not a problem: "A game of step-ball fills the bill perfectly."

The old homes lined each side of the street in Craze's neighborhood. Craze's house, located midway in the block, sat directly across the street from a "Greek Revival" home. Craze's house looked completely different: a tall, thin, three-story "Victorian" painted white with kelly green paint around the windows.

"That house looks just like a southern mansion with those four large pillars holding up the roof of the porch…not that I ever saw a real one."

The neighbor's terrace stood fifteen feet above the street, making the steps a perfect place for a game of step ball. The four huge trees on top of the terrace added to the southern mansion touch. Craze's terrace stood only four feet above the street, the perfect height for a home run ball when Craze threw the ball just right against the edge of the neighbor's step. While sitting on the curb and chewing, Craze thought about the two choices in life his Grandpa had suggested: "Craze, I think you'd make a great president of the United States or…left-handed pitcher for the *St. Louis Cardinals.*"

"First my parents tell me I'm going to college so I can get a better job, and now Grandpa tells me that I've got two jobs to pick from . . . Easy choice. I'll be a lefty for the *Cards.*"

Snapping back to reality, and the game, Craze went through his checklist:

"Okay, wads of gum, tennis ball, glove, *Cardinals* hat, and baseball cards…But, my fingers are still sticky, oh well."

After flipping over his first card, Craze stood in the middle of the street, and announced, out loud, to the imaginary crowd, "Now pitching for the *St. Louis Cardinals*, left-handed pitcher, The Great Craze… Holy Cow."

"Lefty" let the ball go and it struck the neighbor's steps. Now screaming, Craze yelled as he chased the ricocheted ball down, "FLY BALL deep to center field and the center fielder is on the move. He goes up against the wall and steals a homer, 'HOLY COW! WHAT A SENSATIONAL CATCH.'"

Craze continued playing his game against the steps, until something interrupted him.

Craze shouted, "The wind-up and the pitch…"

Stopped in his tracks by the noise blaring out of "the mansion," Craze stopped before throwing the ball and listened.

"What the heck is that; something's wrong with that music?" he thought. A record player blasted a rock and roll tune with a guy shouting the words, "Log cabin, maple syrup…!" followed by an up-tempo rock and roll beat.

At that point, the neighbor kid, who lived in the "mini mansion," started beating on some drums.

"What's he doing? It's all wrong!" Craze tried the wind-up and the pitch...but the drums coming out of the house stopped him cold.

"It's just not right," and Craze somehow knew it. "I can't stand it."

Craze instinctively knew that the beat played by his neighbor did not fit, and it drove him Crazy.

"Somehow, the pieces of this puzzle don't fit. It's all out of kilter."

Craze's family sometimes listened to music in the car, and his mom played *Perry Como* and *Dean Martin* music on the record player at home. But he never paid much attention to music.

"Now, I've lost track of the ballgame score."

Craze took a break from his game and paid more attention to the banging. Holding the ball in his glove, he felt the beat that his drumming neighbor evidently did not. He threw his glove and tennis ball down on the sidewalk and headed up the stairs that, moments ago, had been part of his ball field. "That's it! I've gotta straighten him out!"

The beat to "Log Cabin, Maple Syrup" etched into his mind as he approached the front door; his mission: "Something is completely wrong; that kid's wrecking the beat to that lousy song, and I'm gonna stop it right now."

Somehow, Craze instantly knew that the song itself did not matter, but keeping the right rhythm to any song did matter. He had to stop the infraction before he went completely insane. Craze knocked on the front door, and the guilty party, the neighbor kid, answered. Craze brushed past the kid and entered a room where he noticed a makeshift drum set made up of two congas and an old metal-rimmed ashtray stand the neighbor used for a cymbal. A record player sat on the table next to the set-up. His neighbor held a pair of drumsticks, which Craze had never held before. He grabbed the sticks out of the kid's hands and ordered, "Hey, put that stupid song on the record player again."

Obeying Craze's demand, the kid started "Log Cabin, Maple Syrup" from the beginning. Craze thought about what he had heard in his head outside just moments before. After only seconds, he clearly heard the drum parts. He thought, "Wait, there's the snare and the bass drum parts…and a cymbal part that rides over the top of the music…down bass, up snare, down bass, up snare, 1, 2, 3, 4."

For some reason unbeknownst to Craze, the drum parts clearly stood out in his mind and seemed louder than the rest of the musical parts coming out of the record player.

"1, 2, 3, 4, the one and three-beat is the bass. The two and four beat is snare–drum; down bass, up snare. Wait, there's more… One beat, bass-drum, TWO beats, snare, then one beat bass-drum and only ONE beat, snare…now the cymbals, 1, 2, 3, 4, 1, 2, 3, 4…Hey, start that song over again."

Drum parts flowed through Craze's veins, and right into his soul…and from that point on, the BEAT never left him.

Craze left the house and walked back down the steps; but so many things had changed since the last time he saw them. The pitcher's mound turned back into the street and the imaginary baseball field had disappeared. Craze picked up his stuff and headed for his front door. In that life-changing moment, Craze thought, "Somehow, I just got a gift and didn't even ask for it . . . Well, I guess the *Cards* lost their chance . . . I gotta buy me some drums."

Chapter 2

Long Haired Music

After saving for months—plus money from his thirteenth birthday—Craze bought that drum set for sixty dollars, an old white pearl Ludwig set with a huge 30-inch bass drum.

"Man, that's a lot of dough. That's the most money I ever spent on anything. I was shaking when I handed over that much cash."

Craze set up the Ludwig drums in his bedroom and incessantly practiced, learning rock songs from every record he could get his hands on. He wondered, "I don't know how my parents put up with this constant banging…Oh well, I guess I'll learn how to play 'Satisfaction' tonight."

After a few months of practicing in his bedroom, the kitchen ceiling below Craze's bedroom caved in. Craze understood when his parents made him move his drum set down to the basement. "For 'safety reasons,'" his parents explained.

In their never-ending adventures of exploring their church, Craze and Peter had recently discovered a small room, or more exactly, a large-sized closet. The room contained a small table pushed up against a radiator on the back wall and a chair on each side. The radiator made the small room warm, actually hot,

Figure 3. Craze at age 13.

enough that when they left the "closet," they both had beads of sweat on their foreheads. Shelves containing art supplies occupied each side of the room. Every Sunday morning before Sunday school, the two 13-year-olds met in their newly discovered, nearly perfect secret meeting place for discussions of their previous week's adventures.

Craze and Peter entered the room and took their designated spots on the two chairs. As he always did, Peter grabbed a can of crayons off a shelf before he sat down and placed them in the middle of the table.

"Man, have I got a great idea," he said.

On this particular Sunday morning, Peter busted out with excitement about his new proposal. Before he began, he reached in the can, as he had done every Sunday since the great discovery of their secret room and took out an olive-colored crayon. Peter peeled off the paper wrapper while Craze grabbed a red one and did the same. As they did every Sunday, they both pressed their crayons against the hot radiator and watched them melt down the side and form a small wad of color on the floor below. Craze wondered about the previous week's melted crayons: "I wonder who cleans this mess up anyway? Every Sunday, the melted crayons from last week somehow disappear. Oh well, I guess nobody minds. They probably get paid or something."

Craze grabbed another crayon, a blue one this time, and melted it on top of the same spot where he had melted the red one, creating purple-colored ooze on the floor. Peter broke the silence.

"Man, I told you about the cool new guitar I bought a few weeks ago," he said. "It's light blue and made in Japan; I think that's a good thing. AND, the body is shaped real cool. The distance between the strings and neck make it a little hard to play, but that don't matter, it looks great! What's important is that the guitar looks cool, and this one was cheap enough for me to buy. I can even play it already."

Craze thought, "That makes perfect sense and Peter NEVER lies. He told me a couple of years ago that he was gonna be a classical pianist and in no time at all, he could play that piano like a wildman. Okay, here's my idea."

They both continued sweating, reaching in the can and melting crayons on the red-hot radiator.

"Man wouldn't it be cool to start a combo," Peter said. (An ancient title used at the beginning of the band revolution.) "I can play guitar and sing and you can be the drummer...Craze, think of the chicks. How cool would that be? I can still practice classical piano and play in a band too!"

Craze thought, "I wonder why he doesn't want to play a keyboard; he's so good? Oh well, I guess he thinks playing guitar is cooler. Chicks DO like guitar players better."

The band bug had struck Peter, and now, Craze too.

"Yeah man, I'm all in. Who else could we get? Maybe Dennis would be interested. Joey's out, because he's already in a combo."

Dennis and Joey, fellow piano players, attended the same Sunday school class with Craze and Peter. Peter agreed, melting another crayon, "Yeah man, good idea; let's ask him after class."

Sweating profusely in their sport jackets, ties and slacks, they left the room and entered the classroom down the hall with dreams of stardom swimming in their heads.

𝄞

Peter's dad, a deeply religious man and a country guitar "plunker" himself, beamed with pride over his son's success in the rock music business. Peter's dad viewed this success as his boy carrying on the family torch. Feeding his passion for modern day music, his father listened to "bebop and cool jazz" records on Saturdays while his sons listened along with him.

In the tougher depression days, his dad had even played a little fiddle at square dances, picking up extra cash for the family. Those were dark times that his dad never talked about.

His dad did have one rule: "If you're going to do this, you're going to do it right."

His dad insisted that his son listen to live radio broadcasts of *Albert King* playing "Live from the Blue Note." So the high school boy, along with his younger fifth-grade brother tagging along, got *Albert's* music in their blood.

His dad explained, "You might as well learn from the best."

Peter's problem...PETER WAS NOT THE HONORED OFFSPRING! That honor went to his older brother, Paul. At the time, Peter's passion for music lay elsewhere, specifically in classical piano music. Now this presented a problem. His dad did not understand.

CHAPTER 2

"Why would anybody, especially a fifth grader, want to play classical music?" Not getting it, his shocked dad asked, "So what are you trying to prove by playing that long-haired music?"

The fifth grader had no idea how to answer such a question.

At the age of seven, Peter got his first taste of stardom at an event called "The Splatter Platter Party." The radio station promotion took place at a local swimming pool that featured big name stars. On this particular afternoon, Jerry and the Jesters, Peter's big brother's band, backed up Jerry Lee Lewis and Fabian. Peter innocently stood backstage as Jerry Lee finished his set. Still not on the premises and very late for his cameo appearance, Fabian's crowd grew more and more impatient. Needing a "time killer," the master of ceremonies, a popular disk jockey in town came up with an idea. He walked over to Peter and said in his St. Louis accent, "Hey, kid you want to make two dollars?"

Not one to pass up making a few bucks, Peter responded, "Well sure."

"Okay kid, all you got to do is when I say 'HERE"S FABIAN,' just walk out on stage and take a big bow."

Peter's seven-year-old mind told him, "That's easy enough money ... okay, but give me the cash up front."

Peter collected his cash, and the DJ announced, "Ladies and gentlemen, the one and only Fabian!"

On cue, Peter entered the stage to the welcoming cheers of the audience and took his over-exaggerated bow. Rising up from his bow, Peter's eyes made contact with the angry teenagers as their cheers turned into boos. Peter scurried off-stage, finding safety in a dark corner. *Fabian* finally showed up and saved the day. On his way to the stage and his adoring fans, he stopped and patted the young man in the corner on the head, saying,

"How you doin' kid?"

The unpopular little boy had just suffered his first bad experience in the tough business of rock and roll.

As younger brothers do, Peter followed in some of his big brother Paul's footsteps. By the seventh grade, Peter had two musical interests: he not only loved his "long-haired" piano music, he also got hooked on his older brother's love for Albert King's music. This passion eventually led to Peter's fascination with The British Invasion, and the purchase of his cheap, powder blue Silvertone Guitar sealed the deal.

But his dad never witnessed Peter's successes in both rock and classical music. His father passed away soon after Peter turned 15.

𝄞

Craze and Peter had a problem in launching their rock-and-roll dream. Peter proclaimed, "I'm savin' up for an amp man, but I just don't have enough yet."

Craze replied, "I've got an idea, man. There's a guy named Rod in my class at school who's been talking about his new Silvertone guitar and amp. Let's ask him to be in the band."

Peter licked his chops in anticipation of plugging in his cool shaped "axe" and wailing away.

"Cool man, do it. Get a hold of him and set it up. I'm ready," Peter declared.

Craze contacted Rod at school and proposed the plan. Running home, Craze called Peter and gave him the good news. "He took the bait hook line and sinker. We're getting together next weekend."

The three future rock stars met at Rod's house and began their first practice. Peter plugged in and wailed on his guitar in total ecstasy. Fearing damage to his amp, Rod stopped Peter's exuberance.

"Hey man, turn it down. You're gonna hurt my amp and besides, my mom's gonna get mad."

CHAPTER 2

So Peter respectfully turned down and practice began. Peter suggested several songs.

"Hey man, you know the chords to 'Little Latin Loopy Lou'?"

"Uh, no I never heard of that one…"

"How about 'Johnny Be Good,' or 'In the Midnight Hour'? They're cool songs."

"No, I've heard them, but I don't know how to play either one."

Peter suggested song after song but Rod, the supposed guitar player, had either never heard of them or did not know how to play them.

Finally Peter said, "Well, I'll tell you what, I'll start a song and you try to follow along, okay? Craze, count off 'Louie, Louie.'"

As the trio attempted different songs, every time Rod looked away, Peter slowly turned himself up and Rod down, drowning out Rod's mistakes. Rod lagged behind on every song while Peter adjusted the amp at every opportunity. Rod spent the afternoon distracted by unsuccessfully concentrating on his guitar playing while Peter and Craze got their first taste of playing in a band. The practice ended with the three guys congratulating each other on a great rehearsal.

Peter and Craze left Rod's house each individually thinking, "That guy doesn't have any idea how to play the guitar." But Peter and Craze got to wail for the first time and it felt good.

The three got together a couple more times with the same results. Craze and Peter practiced, ignoring Rod's floundering efforts. But Craze and Peter learned a valuable lesson in these practice sessions. They realized they might be on to something. They knew they clicked together perfectly and both knew they wanted to continue playing together. They also knew Rod eventually had to go, but for the time being, he had the amp.

To make money, Peter taught piano lessons. Craze followed suit and started teaching drum lessons to a few of his younger brother's friends. Craze thought, "If other kids want to pay us for music lessons, who are we to turn them down? As long as they pay, and they're happy with the results, who are we to deny them?"

Peter dug deep in his soul and pocket for an answer: "Without that precious amp, we're stuck."

Peter gathered his strength and approached his parents. "Mom and Dad, I just don't have enough money to buy this amp. If you loan me the money, I promise I'll pay you back."

After an evening of discussion, his parents came back with their proposal: "We'll loan you the money if you set up a payment plan and promise to stick to it."

Peter agreed and the next day, with the dough in his pocket, he went to Sears and bought the coveted Silvertone amp. The next step, a tough one: call Rod and inform him that his services were no longer needed.

Dennis, a keyboard player, attended the same Sunday school class as Craze and Peter. After the "lousy drummer's" family had moved out, Dennis's family had moved into the "mansion" house across the street from Craze. Dennis's family moved constantly because his father worked for the railroad. After living in the house for a year, his dad got transferred again. But Dennis, two years older than Craze, stayed behind and moved in with Craze's family until he finished his last two years of high school.

Craze asked his new roommate, "Hey Dennis, how close are you to buying your keyboard and amp?"

In his quiet, mild-mannered, southern voice, the keyboard player replied, "Real close Craze. I got the dough saved. I just got to go get it."

Dennis did not only talk slow, he did everything slow, so the slow purchase did not surprise Craze.

"Well, you know me and Peter have been practicing. We thought you might be interested joining the band. But, you'll have to spring for the keyboard pretty soon if you're interested."

As he chomped at the bit waiting for an answer, Craze thought, "Well I think that approach was tactful enough."

Dennis slowly responded, "Well Craze that might be fun. Let me think about it."

"What kind of answer was that?" Craze mused.

After a few minutes, Dennis responded, "You know what, Craze, that does sound like fun. I'll do it. I'll just have to get around to picking the stuff up."

With that slow but positive answer, Craze and Peter finally filled another piece of the band puzzle ... after Dennis finally got around to buying his keyboard and amp.

𝄞

The process of choosing a bass player did not take long. After experimenting with a few guys, they picked the best-looking guy, a kid named Steve. The tall, dark and handsome bass guitar player looked cool and acted cool. AND, as he stood beside the other three guys with his bass strapped on, Craze thought, "We got us a chick magnet!"

But all this "drawing power" came with a few minor problems. He DID own his own equipment, a critical requirement, but Steve really DID NOT know how to play bass guitar. While discussing this problem, Peter quickly volunteered, "Problem solved, man! I teach kids how to play every day. What's one more? And he IS better than Rod."

The band had filled the critical position of "chick attracter."

𝄞

With great enthusiasm, the four band members gathered at Peter's house for their first rehearsal. Like peacocks in a field, the room immediately filled with "cool displays" and noise, as each "musician" showed off his amazing talents. But all the "impressive peacocking" went unheard because nobody paid attention to the others. Riffs from a thousand different songs filled the air, until Peter ordered the room quiet. Peter proclaimed, "Shhhh, let's play 'Louie Louie.'"

In unison, the guys agreed, "Yeah man, cool."

Craze clicked his sticks, "Okay ready? 1, 2, 3, 4."

Paul, Peter's older brother, sat in the background as the first song began ... well, attempted song ... but chaos better described the racket. While playing the "song," the band faced Paul, seeking his approval.

Paul had taken an interest in his younger brother's band and offered his help; the guys readily agreed. Paul had already come up with their name, *The Vegas,* and had made a real cool black bass drum head with the same words written in silver glitter. The guys in the band agreed. "This is the coolest thing we've ever seen."

Armed with their cool new bass drum head, the combo members readied themselves for taking over the world. After a few bars of "Louie Louie," mentor Paul jumped up from his perch in the corner and barked,

"Stop, stop, stop. Hold on a minute. Why don't we start by tuning first? Then, pick a key, you're all playing in a different key."

Settling down from the shock of being stopped, they agreed, thinking in unison, "Well, okay, if you insist."

Paul continued, "Remember this. Don't EVER play out of tune, and by the way, don't sing out of tune either. Both are signs that you don't know what you're doing. If you're out of tune on stage, don't wait for the end of the song; tune up right away, or you'll ruin the song. And by the way, tune up quietly and spare your audience the agony of seeing you tune. Do it quietly and don't draw attention to yourself."

Craze thought, "Paul got all that information from twelve bars? He's a genius! Man, this might be harder than we thought."

"Now remember, stop playing if you're out of tune." Paul stated in a much milder tone.

The band struggled through another version of "Louie, Louie," but Steve, the bass guitar player, had problems hitting the right notes. Peter patiently assisted Steve one more time, showing him where to push the strings on his bass. Then they attempted several other songs, like "Little Latin Loopy Lou," "Satisfaction" and Craze's favorite, "Wipe Out." The band labored through each song while Peter patiently helped Steve. After a couple of hours, they ended the rehearsal exhausted.

As they packed, Paul, a well-experienced musician, stepped forward and spoke more words of wisdom. "Now go home and rest. But before you leave, I suggest that you make plans for your next rehearsal. Sit down after packing and figure out the specific songs that you're going to work on next time. Before the next rehearsal, everybody practice your parts so that you don't waste valuable rehearsal time. And Peter…TELL THEM WHICH KEY."

"Here's something else I suggest you do. Watch how the big boys do it and borrow some of their ideas. They've spent lots of time and money on every aspect of their show. They've already figured out most of this stuff already. So, observe and learn."

Craze thought, "I'm not exactly sure what he's talking about."

As per Paul's recommendations, the group dutifully agreed on tunes for their next practice and went home more exhausted.

The next rehearsal began the same as first, with the room spinning out of control as each member played their newly learned parts thinking, "Man I'm cool, I'm really impressing the guys and the chicks are really digging me now."

With nobody listening, just wailing, Paul interrupted, "Guys, guys, stop, stop."

When things calmed down, mentor Paul gently continued, "God gave most of you guys in this room a gift, and you're abusing it. Treat it with respect. Quit this nonsense and start rehearsing."

With Paul's assistance, the guys actually learned how to rehearse. The disciplined rehearsals actually produced complete songs. At one such rehearsal, Paul talked about bands in general.

"All it really takes to play in a band is rhythm, enthusiasm, good taste and the ability to follow directions. You'd be surprised how many people lack these simple abilities. After that, talent and determination will decide how far some of you go in the music business."

The guys in the band all sat pondering these words, thinking, "I guess we'll find out."

𝄞

After several rehearsals, and Paul's valuable mentoring, *The Vegas* dubbed themselves ready for public scrutiny.

Paul gathered the troops for their final pow-wow before their first gig, a talent show at school. "Let's sit down and have a talk before you guys leave; there are some final things you need to know."

Pacing back and forth, he seemed as nervous as a father sending his children off to school for the first time:

> "You guys have worked hard and paid attention and I'm proud of your progress. First of all, remember what I said about playing out of tune. And Peter, do not sing flat. Be sure to tune before you start and for heaven's sake if you tune between songs, don't let the audience see or hear you do it. Also, don't mess around practicing the next song between songs. Those distractions cheapen your performance.

Make a set list of songs for the gig just like you did for rehearsals. It's okay to take requests, but go back to the list after you play the request. Make sure you mix up fast and slow songs to give your performance some variety. By the way, Peter, speak clearly and loudly so the crowd hears what you have to say. If you tell a joke or funny story and you guys laugh without them hearing it, it'll look like you're laughing at them.

Also, don't just play the notes; play them with your soul, and show your passion to the audience. Finally, this entire endeavor is about the audience. Pay attention to their reaction; they'll let you know what they like and don't like. This is not about what you like; it's about what they like. Now go out there and tear them up."

Exhausted and drained, Paul left the room. Craze thought, "Wow, we're only playing one song!"

Figure 4. *The Vegas* with Steve, Peter, Craze, and Dennis.

Earlier, the band had picked the perfect song for the talent show. Peter spoke up, "Hey man, we got the perfect song sitting right in out laps . . .'Bald Headed Woman' by the *Kinks*. It isn't our best song, but it sure is funny, I guarantee a win!"

The band had convinced themselves that the audience would "roll in the aisles."

That night at the show, the band listened to the other acts. With a concerned look on his face, Peter watched a girl playing a Chopin piece on the piano. Leaning over to Craze, Peter said, "Man, she's pretty good, but classical music ain't gonna beat rock and roll ... no way."

Somewhat comforted by Peter's words, Craze and the band took their positions on stage. They confidently played "Bald Headed Woman" and left the stage, thinking that they had won.

"It's in the bag. We'll just stick around and collect our trophy."

"And the winner is…" the girl who played Chopin.

As the air went out of their tire of confidence, Craze thought, "Maybe we should have picked a good song. I guess serious never beats funny."

Crushed, they left the building wondering what had gone wrong.

Dennis, the keyboard player, hung up the phone in the kitchen and headed upstairs to the third floor attic. Being roommates with Craze and sharing the attic, he walked through his room and entered Craze's room. Craze sat in a chair admiring the new Hendrix poster that he had just mounted in a blank space on the wall. The tongue-and-groove wood angled ceiling could barely be seen through all the stuff hanging on the ceiling. Craze took great pains decorating his room with the best cool band stuff that he could find.

Dennis sat down on the floor in front of Craze on a cheap, but still cool, Indian rug. Dennis spoke slowly, "Hey man, I got something I have to tell you. That was the *T. R. and The Nomads* on the phone and they asked me to join their band. Craze, I don't want to hurt you guys, but I got to take it. I'd be nuts not to, don't you think?"

Craze thought, "Man, *The Nomads* are the best band around."

Stunned by the news, but understanding his predicament, Craze came out of his shock and agreed with Dennis. "Yeah man, you'd be insane not to take the offer."

Years later, Peter wondered, "Man, why didn't they pick me instead of Dennis?"

Craze and Peter…and for that matter Dennis . . . .all knew how much better Peter played the keyboard than Dennis. Craze calmly informed Peter, "Obviously they didn't even know that you played the keyboard. All they ever heard you play was the guitar."

"Oh, I never thought of that."

Secretly ecstatic about the way things had worked out, Craze thought, "What would life have been like without Peter? Thank God they never heard him play piano."

With Dennis out of the picture, and booked gigs, Craze and Peter found themselves in a pickle. A new keyboard player became their top priority, and one who could afford buying the expensive equipment was "hard to come by." At the same time, the band got kicked out of Peter's house.

"Sorry man, but my mom says the loud music is driving her nuts."

Saving Peter's mom's sanity, rehearsals moved to Craze's basement. The move also left them without Paul's mentoring.

Peter explained, "He said he didn't mind helping us as long as he didn't have to go anywhere."

Now on their own, Craze and Peter found a guy named Skinner who "kind of played keyboard" but had plenty of cash. The guys found out that he had a rich uncle who would buy him just about anything, including band equipment.

Craze and Peter rationalized, "Easy decision! We've crossed that bridge with Steve, the bass guitar player, and it kind of worked out, so why not solve this keyboard problem the same way with Skinner as our keyboard player? I'll teach them both at the same time and that will save me time ... problem solved!"

With the addition of Skinner, and to their surprise, Craze, Peter and Steve now faced the strange world of "redneck." Besides band equipment, keyboard Skinner's uncle had bought him a '56 canary yellow hot rod Plymouth, so trips to rehearsal and gigs turned into "street races." Every stop sign turned into a starting line. Skinner challenged fellow drivers, young and old, male or female, to a race, revving up his engine and giving them the stink-eye.

Skinner's uncle had *The Vegas* play at a party at his house out in the country. After their first set, and a few drinks on Skinner's uncle's part, he took the band out to his garage and showed then his '62 Chevy Dragster. It turned out that his uncle was a professional racecar driver. His uncle said, "You guys want to go for a ride?"

Volunteering for the others, Craze replied, "Is the Pope Catholic? Of course we want to go for a ride."

So they all jumped into the racecar, Craze taking the seat behind the uncle with Peter in the middle and Steve on the other side. Uncle said, "Let's fire this baby up."

The guys, except for Skinner, had never witnessed anything like that sound before, an explosion on wheels deafening the guys even more than any instrument ever had. Pulling out of the garage and burning out several times, the so-called "ride" began. They innocently putted down the road for a couple of blocks until they reached the hilly outer road, which ran alongside an interstate highway.

Uncle stopped the car as if he was at a starting line and said, "Hold on, we're gonna light this baby up."

All of a sudden, the rocket launched, throwing everybody back in their seats. Craze desperately thought, "We're all gonna die."

The hills now acted like a seesaw with the racecar going up and down, up and down. Straining to lift his head, Craze looked up just in time to see the speedometer go over 140. After that, Craze gave up and let his head fall back into the seat.

Peeking out the window with one eyeball, Craze watched the cars pass on the highway, thinking, "They look like they're sitting still, parked."

The guys lost a little innocence that night.

For a while, Skinner solved the keyboard problem. The band played the gigs and made some money. But Peter found himself stretched to the limit. He soon realized that he had bitten off more than he could chew.

"Craze, covering my own guitar parts and vocals, and teaching two other people isn't gonna work, man. My schoolwork, my classical music lessons and my church responsibilities are all suffering. It's killing me. We have got to do something, and quick. I could see my parents yanking me out of the band and that's unthinkable."

The miscalculation had to end. The issue became: "somebody has to go; bass guitar player, or keyboard player, BUT WHO?"

Chapter 3

The Volcano and Boats Birthday Party

With no keyboard players available, the stink eye had turned on the bass player Steve.

"Peter, I've been checking around and word has it that an old friend of mine and classmate named Lawder plays a pretty mean bass. I knew that he played cello, but I didn't know that he had switched to bass guitar. He invited me to hear his band at their next practice. I'll check him out and if he's as good as they say he is, I'll try to hook him."

Hearing music blaring from inside, Craze arrived on his bike outside his fellow classmate and friend Knight's house. As he entered the practice room, along with Lawder and Knight, Craze noticed another fellow classmate and friend, Boat, playing the drums. Knight stood playing guitar, Boat sat playing the drums and of course Lawder took his place along side the drum set playing bass guitar.

After listening to a few tunes, Craze thought, "Lawder's as good as advertised; he's a natural. I think we're better than these guys, so we might have a chance. Now, I've got to figure out how to steal him."

After practice, Craze approached Lawder and asked, "Hey Lawder, my band is practicing at my house next week. You want to come over and join us? I think you'll have fun."

CHAPTER 3

"Sure man, why not."

Craze thought, "Well, that was easier than I expected. Now we've just got to sway him."

That next week, Lawder showed up for practice and fit in perfectly. The rest was history; Craze and Peter knew that they had found their man.

Unfortunately for Steve and luckily for Skinner, Steve was out. Craze and Peter had the difficult job of telling Steve the bad news. Craze and Peter made the call and "the deed was done." Sadly, Steve had become a friend, but "just good-looking" no longer filled the bill. Lawder's talent could not be overlooked.

Now practicing in Craze's basement, with Paul's mentoring ended, Lawder learned his parts fast and immediately fit in. Besides playing bass guitar, Lawder also added a new dimension to the band: perfectionist. Lawder insisted on every "T crossed and I dotted" before a song hit the stage. But, like all of the guys in the band, Lawder too had a story.

All the other students had gone home. Lawder's mind longingly wandered back to last summer when he, Craze, and a fellow buddy spent time together riding their bikes to McDonalds and putt putt. But Lawder's face did not show an expression of pleasure. Instead, his expression reflected his concern over the fact that his teacher waited for him in the room at of the end of the hallway. She wanted to discuss his failing grades. Recently, Lawder's dad had gone to work one day and never came home. He just vanished into thin air, never to be seen again.

Lawder thought, "So how do I explain that?"

With his cello strapped over his shoulder, Lawder made his way to his classroom door and his waiting teacher. Lawder listened to his own footsteps echoing in the wide, tall, perfectly polished hallway floors of Avery School as he made his way to the executioner's chamber. How does a sixth grader explain mad, hurt, and alone?

"What can I say to her? Nobody understands what I'm going through. I hate it here."

𝄞

The class had been through a lot together. At Avery, the teachers kept their students for two years, so, by the second year, Miss Kitamura knew her students well. The class also knew her well. Miss Kitamura proved her devotion to her students through her kindness and understanding. And she did not hide her excitement when she experienced new things in her life. The class had fun watching their Hawaiian teacher witness these new things. They enjoyed watching her fascination with seeing her first snowfall through the windows of classroom. Teaching stopped and the class gathered at the windows so she could experience the large snowflakes falling to the ground. The class also witnessed other firsts in her life, like her first tornado warning drills, leaves dropping off of trees in the fall, and other life events not found in Hawaii.

Lawder thought, "I love watching somebody else see things for the first time. She gets so excited. She's learning too, so it's like we're the teachers."

Bottom line, the class trusted her. Lawder trusted her and liked her very much, but that affection did not supply the words for his dilemma.

He thought, "She can't possibly understand why my grades are bad, nobody can, except for maybe my mom."

Lawder and Craze loved Miss Kitamura, and Lawder did not blame her for any of his difficulties. Aware that Lawder had skipped a grade after testing by the new school, Miss Kitamura wondered about the judgment of that move.

Lawder thought, "I think getting up every morning and watching PBS on TV helped me skip a grade. I love that time by myself. I get lost in those stories about other places and things around the world. It's like they're talking directly to me."

Miss Kitamura knew that Lawder had transferred from a much less prominent inner city school, but the Avery School tests proved him capable of skipping a grade. At age 8 and in the 3rd grade, Lawder's family moved to this middle class neighborhood from a poor black neighborhood in the inner city of St. Louis. Lawder lived a happy life there, getting along with all the kids, black or white. Lawder knew skipping a grade had not created the problem, but she didn't, and his sixth grade brain had no way of explaining his dilemma.

Besides the disappearance of his father, Avery itself had become a painful place for him. Lawder felt others in his class looked down on him because he came from the inner city. Certain kids made fun of Lawder, especially the twin boys in his class, calling him things like "white trash" and "n…lover." Others mocked him and joined in on the name-calling.

Lawder thought, "I don't know why I'm so angry and hurt. I begged my parents to move back and that didn't do any good. So, what do I tell my teacher? Right now, there are more important problems in my life than worrying about reading, writing, and arithmetic."

Finally, Lawder completely lost interest in school. He continued showing up, but his mind focused on the much bigger problems in his life.

Lawder had witnessed racism close up while living back in the old neighborhood. As usual, on Sunday morning, Lawder caught the streetcar going to the Congressional Church located several blocks away from his house. Lawder felt especially excited this day because he had talked two of his African American friends into going with him. They climbed onto the streetcar and paid the 10 cent fare. The three kids happily traveled the distance to the church. Seated on the bus, the three looked out the windows observing the houses and stores along the route.

"This is so fun. I got my buddies going to church with me and boy, will they be excited when they see the inside of my church."

When Lawder and his two friends got to their designated stop, the streetcar halted, and the three innocent kids got off. They made their way up the wide, tall steps and into the large, impressive building. They entered through the massive wooden doors exposing the enormous interior. After a second or two, their eyes adjusted to the light. In front of them, stood the massive, regal interior filled with religious symbols. People's faces also slowly came into their view. Many in the congregation had turned their heads and watched the boys enter.

Walking down the aisle to find a seat, the boys noticed the surprised and angry stares from the exclusively white faces of the seated parishioners. Some whispered while hiding their mumblings behind their hands.

Lawder thought, "They look mad, I wonder what happened?"

Already feeling uncomfortable, Lawder overheard one comment, "What are those two blacks and that 'white trash' kid doing in here? Who do they think they are? Somebody needs to get them out of here."

Now halfway down the aisle and scared, Lawder and his two friends felt like running. Then, they noticed a large white lady ahead of them, who stood up and signaled, "Over here, come sit with me."

Relieved, they followed the lady's instructions and sat down next to her. She protectively put her arms across top of the pew, surrounding them with her safety. After church, scowling faces from the congregation followed them as the lady escorted them to the streetcar stop. She waited with the boys until the streetcar pulled up.

As the three scared kids boarded, she said, "Don't worry about them. Come back any time. I'll make sure nothing happens to you."

Feeling safe in the streetcar, the kids finally caught their breaths. Although somewhat comforted by her words, the three vowed never to return.

𝄞

Lawder waited in the hallway, lost in his thoughts. He snapped back to reality when his teacher invited him into the room.

"Come in Lawder."

Miss Kitamura, small in stature, and a giant in sensitivity, asked, "Lawder, you're so much better than your math grades reflect. You're not keeping up with your other classmates and I know you're smarter than that. What can I do to help you?"

Lawder sat speechless and uncomfortable, thinking, "I don't want to be mean, but what can I say?"

To no avail, Miss Kitamura patiently waited for an answer. Finally, after several awkward moments of staring into each other's faces, she spoke, "Well Lawder, I wish you would let me help you. Just remember, my door is always open if you ever feel like talking."

Excused from the meeting, Lawder left the room, picked up his cello and other belongings and retraced his echoing footsteps back down the same hallway.

𝄞

Abandoned by his dad, Lawder and the remainder of his family felt alone. Struggling with their impossible situation, Lawder thought, "The only good thing to come out of this is I that don't have to watch my older brother take beatings from my dad all the time." But for some reason, his older brother started beating Lawder on a regular basis.

His older brother would shout, "Don't touch my guitar" or "I told you not to play that damn piano," followed by closed-fisted punches to the middle of Lawder's back.

One such encounter took place in Lawder's front yard. His much bigger and stronger older brother landed punches. Holding up his arms in defense, Lawder backed up. While fending off the blows, Lawder took a swing and blacked out. When he came to, Lawder realized that he now stood over his brother in a self-protective stance, his fists up, and ready to take on any more blows. His brother lay on the sidewalk and gasping for air. Apparently Lawder's lucky blow struck right in the middle of his brother's chest, sending his brother to the ground. His panting brother got up and as he made his way up the steps and into the door, he turned to Lawder and said, "So now you think you're tough…well, we'll see about that later."

To Lawder's relief, his older brother finally joined the Marine Corps and the beatings ceased. But the older brother's departure left the rest of the family—Lawder, a younger brother, and his mom—completely alone and fending for themselves. With the remaining family members now in deep crisis, Lawder's mom did the only thing she could do; she took on the additional domestic responsibilities and found a full-time job. Even though his father had left an old car behind, Lawder watched his mom walk to and from work every day because she feared learning to drive so much. Lawder worried about his mom, who had the overwhelming chore of raising two boys alone, "Why didn't he stay and help? Coward, sneaky coward…"

CHAPTER 3

With mixed emotions, Lawder thought, "I'd take the beatings if it meant my mom would get some help."

Lawder felt backed into a corner. Subconsciously, he created a perilous way of dealing with his insecurity; he had terrible temper tantrums. When antagonized beyond his boiling point, Lawder sometimes blacked out. After coming out of his trance, he did not remember what had just happened. The physical signs reared their ugly heads with his ears getting red first, followed by his face turning red just before he exploded like a bomb, thrashing out at anything in his way.

With all that said and done, his brother did distinguish himself in the Marine Corps, first as a helicopter crew chief in Viet Nam and then two years as an Honor Guard stationed at the White House. Lawder acknowledged that turn of events quietly.

𝄞

With the after-school counseling over, a relieved Lawder walked down the hallway mumbling under his breath and thinking, "So, how could I possibly explain my life to Miss Kitamura? And why should I want to have anything to do with school anyway? I hate this school and some of the people in it. Distant piano music suddenly interrupted Lawder's thoughts.

"What's that? I've never heard anything like it."

The unusual piano music immediately cleared his mind of its uncomfortable thoughts, and for a moment, his difficulties vanished. Somehow, this music had pierced his inner soul as nothing had before. Following the sound down the hallway and to the basement, the music had drawn Lawder to a familiar place: the music room across from the gym. Lawder had spent many hours in the room taking cello lessons. Thankfully, the school had provided free classes and free access to a cello; otherwise Lawder's family would have never been able to afford the lessons.

The open door lured him in. Lawder quietly entered the familiar room. He recognized the short, middle-aged, African American janitor sitting at the piano. Hoping the janitor had not noticed him, Lawder silently took a seat in the corner so he could observe more of this performance. To Lawder's pleasure, the song continued until the end. After the song ended, the janitor raised his eyes from the keyboard and turned his gaze toward the young boy huddled in the corner. A slight apprehension came over Lawder for a moment. "I hope I'm not bothering you. Please play more."

The janitor spoke in a mild calming voice, "You like that music boy?"

Lawder meekly shook his head, "yes."

"Well if you don't know already, that's called 'stride,' a kind of the blues/jazz thing you might say."

The janitor turned back to the keys and played more stride music. Extremely pleased with the outcome, the young boy settled in his chair and enjoyed the rest of the janitor's piano concert.

Finishing up his last song, the janitor said, "Come back any time, I don't mind."

So in the coming days, Lawder looked forward to the mind-clearing sessions with the janitor. Quietly sitting and listening, the music temporarily erased all the bad thoughts from his brain. Lawder relaxed. One afternoon, the music started particularly late. The janitor explained, "Sorry son, I had more chores than usual and as you know, the work comes first."

The time got later and later as they both got lost in the music emerging from the janitor's heart. Lawder thought, "Man, this is the life. Some day, I gonna play something like stride and make people feel happy just like I do now."

They lost track of the time and the world around them disappeared, as they peacefully enjoyed the moment.

CHAPTER 3

Suddenly, Lawder's mom rushed into the room. "What are you doing; what's going on? I've been worried sick. You didn't come home for dinner and I've been looking all over for you."

Lawder immediately thought, "Oh no, now I've ruined everything; the one thing I like about this school and I've screwed it up."

Hastily, the janitor came to Lawder's rescue and apologized to Lawder's mom, explaining, "I'm so sorry, the boy is just listening to me play the piano. He really seems to enjoy my playing and I saw no harm in his listening."

After calming down and observing the scene, Lawder's mom appeared satisfied and relieved with the janitor's explanation. The janitor apologized once more as Lawder and his mom departed the room and went home. That night Lawder lay in his bed depressed by the thought that he had destroyed his chances of ever hearing the janitor play again.

The next day, Lawder dragged himself down the hall still depressed by last night's debacle, thinking, "Well I guess that's over."

At the end of the hall, the janitor stood bent over, sweeping the floor with a large-sized dust mop. As Lawder passed by, the janitor took notice of him, rose up and pulled Lawder aside. The middle-aged man softly spoke out, "Boy if you're still interested in listening to my music, meet me after school in the music room and we'll talk about it."

Lawder went through the school day wondering what the janitor had in mind.

After school, Lawder made his way to the music room and waited. Finally, the janitor entered and said, "I've got a deal for you. I called your mom and we agreed that we can't have you coming home so late. But, she also agreed with my new plan. If you help me with my chores, I can get done early and the rest of my time will be devoted to you. While you're listening to me play, I'll also buy you a Coke for your labor."

Lawder happily agreed to the deal. From that day on for the rest of the semester, the two met after school at the janitor's closet. With his mother's approval, Lawder and the janitor cleaned the rooms and hallways. Then, the janitor and Lawder, armed with his coveted 8-ounce Coke bought in the teacher's lounge, made their way to the music room where each took their assigned places. The janitor took his place at the piano and played stride, while Lawder slowly sipped away all the recent darkness in his life.

Looking back, Lawder told Craze, "I knew after those afternoons listening to the janitor's stride that music was going to be with me the rest of my life."

🎼

"Let's do it one more time," Lawder insisted.

Lawder had introduced a new concept to *The Vegas*: "Practice a song until you're sick of it," he theorized. "On stage we don't need to be thinking about what comes next in the song. By then, we need to focus our attention on the crowd, and the only way to get that point is by playing a song until we're sick of it. From now on, we attack songs at practice. Let's do it again."

The band repeated the song.

"Okay, let's do it one more time; this time pay attention to the dynamics in the middle of the song."

The band obediently repeated the song.

"Now, this time let's clean up the ending." Lawder insisted on repeating the song several times, each time improving the song by making minute musical suggestions.

Exhausted and tired of the song, Craze suggested, "Hey man, let's take a break or do a different song."

Lawder glared at Craze, "So you're tired, you big baby. Well, at least that means you're getting there. From now on, we're taking these songs to a higher level. So, get used to it." Craze cowered and again obeyed Lawder's command. Besides, Peter agreed with Lawder, so "that was the end of that" for Craze's complaint. Peter counted off the song one more time, "One, two, three, four...."

So, Peter joined forces with Lawder as "sticklers for perfection." Together they successfully nurtured *The Vegas* out of puberty and, using their formal training as a template, they transformed the band into a mature musical force on stage. Their motto became: "Practice every detail of a song until you can play it in your sleep or it ain't ready."

Peter and Lawder had completely different methods of getting their points across. On one hand, Peter studiously laid back and pondered every detail. If he calmly said, "Shhhh..." or especially, "That really makes me mad," that meant he had

Figure 5. *The Vegas* with Peter, Lawder, Skinner, and Craze.

reached his boiling point, so stop doing whatever you were doing. And Peter always got his way simply because.

No question about it, he was always right.

On the other hand, Lawder smoldered like a volcano. The ever-present fuming volcano always glowed just underneath the surface. Not possessing the physique of a "muscle man," Lawder's frame hid his solid mass of muscle well, which ended up taking most of his victims by surprise. Craze described Lawder's legs as "tree stumps."

"They're as big on the bottom as they are on top." Describing his entire body Craze thought, "He's one large muscle ready to flex."

The Volcano could erupt at any time, turning things ugly very quickly. But most of the time, the Volcano gave warning signs. First, the Volcano's ears turned red, then its face got redder and redder starting at the bottom and ending on the top. If the redness reached his forehead, and blew its top, nothing could be done except head for the hills. The law of the band became, "Never, under any circumstances, provoke the Volcano, or somebody might die."

So the band paid very close attention to both guys' signs, the whispering Peter and especially the volcanic Lawder.

Boat, a close friend and fellow classmate of Lawder and Craze, said "Hey Craze, wouldn't it be cool if your combo could play at my birthday party? My mom said that I could pay you $25."

Craze gathered himself in his most businesslike manner and responded, "Well Boat, I think we might be available. Let me check my calendar and talk to the guys. I'll let you know."

They parted ways and headed home. Busting at the seams, Craze could not wait to get home and call Peter. He ran all the way home with his brain shouting, "We got a paying gig. We got a paying gig. We got a paying gig...." Craze grabbed the phone on the wall in his large kitchen and dialed Peter's number. Peter's mom answered the phone.

"Hello?"

Breathlessly, Craze replied, "Hi, this is Craze, Is Peter home?"

"Yes Craze, I'll get him."

Waiting for what seemed like forever, Craze paced back and forth in the kitchen, stretching the long phone cord to its limit. "I'm gonna stand here and die of old age waiting for him to pick up the stupid phone. What's going on?"

Peter finally answered, "Hey Craze what's up?" Catching his breath, Craze calmly replied, "What's the coolest thing that could ever happen?"

Peter answered after considering the question for a moment, "I don't know, maybe getting a new guitar and amp?"

"No man, the coolest thing would be getting our first paying gig and guess what? I got one," Craze proudly responded. Craze now shouted in the phone, "We got a paying gig. We got a paying gig. Boat wants us to play at his birthday party, so I got us a paying gig."

In disbelief, Peter pondered, "We got a paying gig." Now more excited, Peter responded, "Wow man, and you're not kidding? That IS cooler; man, we got a lot of work to do."

So, *The Vegas* got their first paying gig...Boat's birthday party. Making the party even better, Boat had invited all of their classmates.

Craze knew Boat from school, but he also hung out with Boat when he visited Craze's neighborhood. Boat once said, "If I'm ever bored, I just come over to Clark Avenue. With that many kids living on the same block (126 to be exact), there's always something going on. Depending on the season, I can always scare up some kind of ball game."

Craze loved watching the ball-launching, shotgun-armed super athlete play sports. Craze also admired Boat's cool manner,

THE VOLCANO AND BOATS BIRTHDAY PARTY 39

"Boat isn't built like an athlete; he kind of reminds me of 'Broadway Joe Namath' when he plays sports."

The birthday party took place about six blocks away from Craze's house in a neighborhood called "The Park," a section of town filled with enormous yards and giant houses. Chauffeured by Craze's dad, the '62 Chevy station wagon loaded with the band members and their equipment pulled into Boat's driveway and headed to his back yard. The long, blacktopped driveway sloped up to the large white painted, black-trimmed "Colonial style" structure located on top of a small hill. The powder blue Chevy followed the blacktop up to the front of an unattached garage and turned right into to a large space located between the garage and the back of the house, where the party preparations took place.

The band set up on a concrete patio built alongside the back of the house overlooking the enormous back yard, which gently sloped down from the back of the house to a tennis court located at the bottom. Plenty of party food, including a big birthday cake, sat on tables in front of the garage doors. A string of multi-colored Christmas lights hung from corner of the garage to the back of the house. Smoking tiki torches with their poles stuck in the ground surrounded the patio. On the opposite side of the patio from the band, small groups of puberty-stricken, well-groomed kids dressed in nice clothes huddled around picnic tables sitting in the grass. Almost every kid did his or her best job of acting cool for the purpose of attracting the opposite sex.

Properly tuned and as well-rehearsed as could be expected by 13-year-olds, the band began their attack on the birthday party crowd. Peter approached the microphone while the other band members took their positions on stage. Peter suddenly realized that his Diet Coke sat on one of the picnic tables on the other side of the patio. "I'm gonna need that later to clear my throat," he said.

CHAPTER 3

Walking past the mic, Peter moved toward his drink, completely forgetting about the cord attached to his guitar. The closer he got to his drink, the more the cord stretched. As he reached for the Diet Coke, the plug attached to his guitar popped out, and recoiled back to the stage. During the trip back to the amp, every time the plug hit the ground, a loud buzzing noise came out of the amp. Finally, the plug came to a rest face down next to the amp, constantly buzzing. Peter grabbed his drink, rushed back to the cord, and replaced the plug in his guitar, causing even a louder buzz. With the buzzing stopped and their ears ringing, the birthday partygoers removed their hands from their ears.

A little disheveled by his misfortune, Peter gathered himself and returned to the mic. He meekly announced to the crowd, "Uh, sorry about that, we are *The Vegas* and our first song is 'Kansas City.'"

Peter signaled Craze to start the first song. Now in the spotlight, Craze nervously clicked his sticks together counting, "One, two..."

One stick flew out of Craze's hand, sailed straight up, and hit him in the head on the way down. Craze got up from behind the drums and retrieved his stick, but not his pride, thinking, "What else can happen?"

Thinking fast, Peter spoke into the mic again, while Craze gathered himself and sat back down behind his drums.

"Uh, sorry about that too...'Kansas City.'"

Embarrassed and avoiding eye contact with any of his friends in the audience, Craze began the count one more time, "One, two, three, four!"

About halfway through the number and feeling better about the situation, Craze humbly raised his head and observed the crowd. "Kansas City" ended with three or four kids clapping. The sparse clapping relieved the massive pressure on stage. Relieved and euphoric over the applause, Craze took a breath and thought, "Man, that's the coolest thing I've ever done."

Starved for more attention and ready for their second song, Boat walked up to the stage and announced, "Guys, my mom says that you have to turn it down. She says it's way too loud. The cops might come."

Confused by this unreasonable request, Craze thought, "What? Wait a minute; if we turn down, they'll be able to hear our mistakes. We just can't do it!"

Although outraged by such a ridiculous demand, the band grudgingly obeyed Boat's mom's orders. While the band played through the rest of their set, the crowd actually danced to a few songs and some even clapped at the end of a few songs. The set ended and the guys confidently mixed with their friends during the break. Peter rustled up a few finger sandwiches and chips while the rest of the band heard comments like, "You guys are great" and "Craze you sounded just like Gene Krupa."

Armed with their friends' compliments, the band returned to the makeshift stage and finished their last set. The band fell

Figure 6. Boat's house.

in love with performing in front of a crowd that day. Craze thought, "Yeah, we made mistakes, but all in all, the evening went well. And best of all, Boat's mom only asked us to turn down four times."

Over the next few months, more gigs came their way; some even paid cash.

The Vegas had a major goal in mind: play a gig at the *Webster Groves YMCA*. To them, a Friday night booking at *The Y* meant the big time. Craze longingly thought, "If we could only play there one time, we could go to our graves in peace knowing that we had made it."

The guys noticed two things that bothered them about most of the bands that played at *The Y*. First of all, most of the bands repeated songs. By now, *The Vegas* had accumulated enough songs for four sets of music. Secondly, most of the bands did not put on a professional show. They did not pay attention to details like clean breaks, dynamics, and messing around between songs. The guys vowed, "*The Vegas* will not let these things happen in our show."

So, with the confidence of a few paying gigs under their belts, Craze set up a tryout.

The big day had finally arrived. Dressed in their coolest clothes, and sweating profusely because *The Y* only turned on the AC for scheduled events, the band nervously set up in the basement. *The Y* required that the tryout bands had to perform three songs in front of five teenage judges. So *The Vegas* picked their three best songs: "Like a Rolling Stone," "Mustang Sally," and "For Your Love." Lawder played to perfection while Peter wailed on his guitar and sang without forgetting the words. Craze beat his brains out on the drums, while Skinner did his best back and forth steps…all in all not a bad performance.

THE VOLCANO AND BOATS BIRTHDAY PARTY

With the trial completed, Craze relaxed behind the drums and thought about their three-song performance. "Well, that went fast. I don't think we made too many mistakes and nothing broke down, so I think we did great…and these judges have to notice the cool stuff we're wearing. All things considered, it turned out great."

After they finished their last song, the four clumsily stood there, not knowing what to do next. One of the judges, an older kid from school seeing the uneasiness, spoke loudly from the table where all the judges sat, "Okay, thank you very much. We'll call you with a decision." The band packed and left the Y. On his way out, Craze, the officially elected leader of the band, passed by the judges' table and passed out the band's newly printed business cards, making sure that they saw his phone number on the card.

"That ought to show them that we're professionals," he thought. "We paid two dollars for a hundred of those babies."

Craze sat behind the drums practicing in his bedroom when his brother entered the room shouting, "I've been hollering from the kitchen. It's for you. It's the Y. You better hurry; they've been waiting for a long time."

His brother turned around and left the room, not realizing the gravity of the moment. Craze flew past his brother on the steps and headed to the kitchen were the phone hung on the wall. He picked up the receiver and choking down his heart, which was now stuck in his throat, announced in his best-faked businessman's voice, "Hello, this is Craze."

The female voice replied, "This is Jody from the *YMCA*. I'm calling to see if your band is available on Friday, June 3rd. We'd like to hire you guys for a performance on that date."

Craze got faint and almost dropped the phone. Recovering, he replied, "Well let me check our schedule."

Grabbing a newspaper left in the kitchen, he ruffled the paper hoping it sounded like a person looking through his notes.

"Yes, yes, that date is still available. Our fee is $100 a night, $25 apiece."

Craze thought, "Why did I say that? That's way too much. They'll never pay that much. Why didn't I let her suggest a price? I've blown it."

After a short pause, she replied, "That sounds very reasonable. We'll see you on the third." Craze hung up the phone and wondered, "Very reasonable? Hum, maybe I didn't charge enough?"

On June 3rd, 1964, their big-time dream came true: they played where all the cool bands played, *The Webster Groves YMCA*. They played with more confidence and polish than they had ever played before. Craze left that night thinking, "I feel like we might actually be getting good."

Their hard work had paid off by making the band one of the most musically polished bands in the area. As the boys got better at their craft, the gigs steadily increased and the pay improved. The band eventually got on the regular rotation of bands playing at the Y. Their attention now focused on professionally performing in front of audiences. Craze thought, "So far, the Y gig IS the greatest experience of my life…but something's still missing… we still aren't cool enough."

Figure 7. Webster Groves YMCA.

Chapter 4

It

"Stage presence, charisma, star power, whatever you want to call it, how do we get it?" Craze thought. "We got the professional music part down, but we don't have that 'wow' factor."

The band knew they needed a killer show to go along with the polished music; a solution would soon land right in their laps.

𝄞

Nearly blind since birth, Eyes casually walked to Billy's house equipped with his always-present Coke-bottle-thick glasses. Without them, everything appeared as a blur; consequently he always wore them. When he looked in a mirror with them, his eyes appeared much bigger than other kids'. So every morning, Eyes put his glasses on first. His big-eyed appearance did not bother him much…first of all because he needed them and secondly his friends never made fun of them.

On this particular Sunday morning, the ten-year-old Eyes navigated his way through the streets of Webster Groves headed to his friend's house. Located several blocks away from Eyes's house, he had plenty of time to think, "So, what IS the big deal; he's black."

Eyes thought about the newspaper article he had read the night before about black people getting beat up in the South. "Besides

Billy, my friend Roger is also black, and he's cool too; so what's the big deal? I guess that I just don't understand humanity."

Eyes and all the kids in his town had no idea that Webster Groves had recently gone through school desegregation, far ahead of many other places in the country. Now Avery, where Eyes attended grade school, included both black and white kids; and the subject of race seldom came up among the kids at school.

But Eyes did notice a difference between his house and theirs; Roger and Billy's houses had music constantly filling the air because their parents constantly played blues music on their record players. Hearing music far in the distance, Eyes continued his thoughts, "That blues music makes their houses feel so much more alive. My house is quiet; except for the classical music coming out of my brother's room, we don't play music, we mostly read books."

He loved books, but without a record player, or TV for that matter, that he could use, his house felt more quiet and studious. Recently his older brother, "The Broker," had purchased a "stereo," the newest thing on the market, which he kept in his room and would not let Eyes touch.

"'The Broker' plays organ music, like *Bach*, real quiet in his room and that doesn't count; it just doesn't move me like the blues." Eyes much preferred the more rough-edged wildness of the blues. As he walked, Eyes thought, "Roger likes *Jimmy Reed*, but I agree with Billy; I'm much more into *The Howlin' Wolf*. Man that *Howlin' Wolf Rocking Chair Album* record tears me up, and that cover, that cover is the COOLEST thing I've ever seen. If they don't play it right away, maybe I'll ask."

Roger's parents kindly allowed Eyes to rifle through their album collection, and looking at the album covers added to his excitement. Eyes loved looking at album covers almost as much as he loved listening to the album itself.

As Eyes walked, the music up ahead got louder and more familiar. Getting more curious about seeing where the music came from, Eyes picked up his pace. As he got closer to the source, he realized that the music he heard came out of the local black Baptist Church. Except for the occasional wedding or funeral, Eyes never actually attended a church. His parents did not go to church, so attending a real church service had not happened in his own life. "Hey, this music really sounds a lot like those blues records that I've been listening to; but hearing it 'live' gives it so much more life...very cool."

He felt electrified by this sound. Now standing on the sidewalk several feet away from a large window on the side of the church, he innocently peered in; what he saw instantly changed his life forever.

A tall, heavy-set black man stood in front of the congregation wailing on a red *Les Paul Gibson* guitar with his accompanying band behind him following his lead. The live sounds rained through Eyes's body, permanently soaking his entire spirit. From that moment on, the resonance of that sound saturated his perspective on life forever. Knocked out by the sound and unable to move, only one word entered his mind. "Wow!"

Sweat poured through the man's straight, black, Ike Turner-like "processed" hair, drizzled down his forehead and off his sweaty cheeks. The man and his band rocked on while the crowd wildly danced, shouting praises like, "Thanks to the Lord." The guitar player had the congregation in the palm of his hands as his soul exited through his fingers. When the music stopped, Eyes stood stunned as if struck by lightning, from the storm he just witnessed. With that lightning bolt scene eternally lodged in his heart, Eyes walked on to Billy's house thinking, "Man, one of these days I'm going to do that to people."

At the age of thirteen, Eyes got his first look at *"The Rolling Stones"* and saw Mick Jagger doing the song *"Not Fade Away."* Bells went off in Eyes's head as he recognized *Bo Diddley's* West African beat. "I heard *"Not Fade Away"* at Roger's house last week and it's the same song."

Figure 8. The church.

Blown away by this new discovery, Eyes concluded, "Oh, so now it's okay for white guys to play the blues and dance around...I'm hip!"

With his "throwing rocks at girls" stage long gone, Eyes knew exactly what he wanted to do with his life now.

Since his newfound interest in blues records, Eyes practically lived at the local record store. He spent hours looking through the volumes of records checking out the hundreds of cool covers. These "Rembrandts" of his world fascinated him and took his mind on a quest, wondering what the record inside actually sounded like. If "the truth be told," sometimes the cover outperformed the record itself.

"It's the dream that matters, not what's actually inside. Just thinking about what might be inside that cover is the fun part."

As he entered the store, Eyes never forgot respectfully to greet the owners, Mr. and Mrs. Gleason, with something like, "Mr. Gleason, how are you today?" or "Mrs. Gleason, you certainly look nice." The couple appreciated his courtesy and gladly welcomed him into their establishment.

Eyes went to the record store so much that, he and the Gleasons became friends. If Eyes saw the owners working on something, he lifted his head up from his latest album cover adventure and willingly offered his help. Eyes would say, "Mrs. Gleason let me take that trash out for you. You have more important things to do."

He helped the Gleasons so much that they decided to pay him. Mr. Gleason said, "Eyes, we've talked it over and we've got an idea. We know that you're not old enough to work behind the counter and use the cash register yet. But since you're already here helping us in other ways, if you're interested, we'd like to hire you on a regular basis; that way you can make a little money for the work you're already doing."

Thinking about his second passion, Eyes thought, "Now I can start saving for a motorcycle."

Eyes had his first job cleaning up the store, and the relationship benefited both parties. Eyes aided in tasks like sweeping up, taking out the trash, and dusting shelves. The Gleasons got the help they needed, and Eyes got paid while hanging out at his most favorite place on the planet. In time, Eyes got his first promotion: stocking the shelves with new albums. When the "boxes of gold" arrived at the store, Eyes got the first shot at witnessing the latest creations in the world of music. When Eyes got old enough, Mr. and Mrs. Gleason allowed him to work behind the counter and use the cash register. Later, Eyes helped manage the store for the now aging couple. His experience at the record store steered him to other jobs in the recording business. Starting out by sweeping those floors at the record shop eventually had a profound effect on Eyes's future.

CHAPTER 4

𝄞

The *Vegas* had joined the regular rotation at the *Webster Groves YMCA*. While performing a show at their favorite venue, something going on in the crowd caught Craze's eye. "Wow, we've got a couple heavy hitters in the crowd tonight," he thought. "I wonder what they're up to?"

During one set, Craze noticed two guys in the crowd; one named Eyes, the lead singer of another band in town named *The King and his Court*, and his friend, Strings, a cool-looking guitar player. Craze knew that Eyes and Strings had great stage presence and cutting-edge ideas about music. He thought, "Man those guys are cool; and Eyes has really got 'IT.' I wish us guys in *The Vegas* could look and act like that."

Eyes played with *The King and His Court*, named after a famous pro softball team. Craze also knew the band was not known for their musical talent, but their front man and singer, Eyes, had become a local celebrity. While watching a *King and His Court* show, Craze thought, "Man, that guy's got 'it.' People are falling all over themselves watching him on stage. Too bad he's way out of our league."

Aware of their tremendous reputations as great showmen, especially Eyes, Craze kept an eye on the two as they sized up *The Vegas*. As the two popular guys stood up front and took in the show, Craze noticed that they paid particular attention to Peter and Lawder.

"They keep whispering back and forth and looking at Lawder and Peter. They seem to be digging their performances …. hmmm, strange." Craze took note of their behavior and kept this event tucked in the back of his mind.

𝄞

Not bothering to knock, Lawder and Peter busted through the front door of Craze's house and sprinted up the steps to Craze's third-floor bedroom. Out of breath from the climb and busting with news, Lawder choked out the words, "Craze that guy Strings called me last night and asked if me and Peter wanted to tryout for a new band with him and Eyes. I called Peter and we rushed right over."

Craze found out later that while attending a "Modern American Music" class at school, Strings and Eyes had become friends as they discovered their mutual passion for the blues. Since then, and because the station came in better at Strings's house, the two spent many late Saturday night sessions sitting beside the radio listening to a Del Rio, Texas, radio station that played obscure old blues tunes. During one of their get-togethers, Strings suggested that they experiment playing some blues tunes with other musicians in town and possibly form a band. Hot about the idea of playing the blues, but cool on the idea of forming a band, Eyes agreed to the proposal.

Fully knowing that Eyes really did not want "to start a band," the guys figured out later that Strings had told Eyes that the gathering "was a jam" and told Lawder it "was a tryout." That way, Strings got the two parties together, and if a band formed, Lawder and Peter would think of him as "the boss." They also found out later that Strings had more conniving ways in his future.

Craze recalled the scene at the Y when Strings and Eyes had paid particular attention to Lawder and Peter's performances. Craze thought, "It all makes sense now, but just how do I fit into this picture? Strings only asked for Lawder and Peter." He decided to hear the guys out before he asked that question.

"We got a plan Craze," Peter explained. "Lawder and I will go over there and try out. If we make it, and when the opportunity strikes, we'll get you in the band too."

Peter and Lawder had become his two closest friends. He grew up with these two guys and believed in their loyalty, so he knew they would try. But the obvious question lurked in Craze's head, "What if that opportunity never comes around?"

He knew better than to ask that question. So Craze bought into the plan. On the other hand, he knew that he had no choice in the matter; they were going to try out with or without Craze's blessing. Craze thought, "They're not gonna pass up this opportunity, and I don't blame them."

On the day of the tryout, Craze, Peter, and Lawder gathered at Craze's house. Peter and Lawder picked up their equipment and headed to Eyes's house a block away. Lawder hollered as he and Peter drove off, "Craze, stay put and wait for us to get back."

Craze obediently waited at home as instructed. After fifteen minutes or so, the phone rang and Craze answered. Lawder shouted, "Craze, get over here right now. The drummer didn't show up."

As fate would have it, on the day of the tryout, the drummer failed to show up. So Peter and Lawder jumped at the unexpected opportunity and suggested that Craze fill in. Apparently Eyes and Strings answered, "Sure, why not?"

So Craze grabbed his already-packed drums and hitched a ride from his mom over to Eyes's house. The rest of the guys continued playing while he set up his drums. Craze could feel the excitement in the air: "Wow, this really sounds good even without drums; Eyes actually looks excited."

After setting up, Craze joined in and the music got even better. Musically, they all performed well and the sound got tighter and tighter the more they played. Craze thought his drum solo in *The Who's* song, "*My Generation*," put him over the top.

"What an amazing feeling!" he thought. "Everybody's doing his job and nobody's lagging behind."

After the tryout, Eyes announced, "Hey you guys, why don't we get together in a couple of days and do this again?"

Strings, thinking of himself as the boss and mad that he did not say it first, chimed in and agreed, saying, "Uh yeah Eyes, that sounds great. Why don't we meet on Saturday? I'll get ahold of everybody when I set up a time."

Arriving back at Craze's house with Lawder and Peter, the three unloaded their equipment. Craze said, "I can't put my finger on it, but something just happened. It's like we all just 'clicked' or something. I think we all felt it; don't you guys agree?"

Thinking about what had just happened, Lawder and Peter shook their heads in agreement.

After a few rehearsals, the guys felt a powerful connection taking place. The bonds that held them together quickly developed into much more than a garage band.

Chapter 5

Invasion

After rehearsal, Eyes said, "You know what? I'm sick of the usual names like *The Ventures, The Sheratons, and The Kingsmen*. I just heard a guy on the radio say, '*This is a Public Service Announcement*' and it struck me. Why don't we call ourselves *The Public Service*? It's something different. What do you guys think?"

The rest of the guys eagerly agreed and thus began the diverse mixture of personalities and talents that jelled into a cohesive unit known as *The Public Service*. Somehow, Craze's business sense, Peter's classical background, Lawder's perfectionism, Strings's coolness, and Eyes's charisma fit like a glove. More importantly, they knew something unique had happened.

On February 9, 1964, less than three months after the assassination of President John F. Kennedy, the world took yet another turn. *The Beatles* invaded *The Ed Sullivan show*, and nothing was the same after that. What followed changed the American youth culture forever. Known as *The British Invasion*, or at first *The English Mod Cult*, British bands poured into the United States. Affected by the movement, half joking and half serious, Eyes and Craze raised their hands and declared, "We dedicate our lives to the preservation of *The English Mod Cult*."

Simply put, they dug the music, dug the spectacle, and dug the individual British guys who performed the music.

Early on, the British bands wore tight-fitting dark suits with no lapels. They wore groomed long hair, thin ties, and high-heeled boots coined "Beatle Boots." The three-inch-high beveled heel Spanish riding boots completed the look. Soon after, the suits disappeared and the garb got wilder and wilder while the hair got longer and longer.

Several other things drew *The Public Service* to *The British Invasion*. First of all, these guys were BANDS, nothing similar to the individual acts like *Fabian* and *Paul Anka* that the "music factories" in the United States cranked out. These "music factory" performers had little to do with what songs they performed or the image they projected. The writers and promo men who showed up in offices from nine to five and mass-produced catchy-phrased songs and dressed them all in similar-looking suits made decisions for them. They all sounded and acted the same.

Exceptions to the single-performer acts existed, like *The Beach Boys* and *The Kingsmen*, but they presented a completely different concept than their counterparts abroad. The British had invented their own unique sound and style completely different than anything experienced in the past. They broke the old unwritten rule about "keeping the music clean and polished" by taking advantage of the natural feedback and distortion created by their guitars and amps. They used the raunchy new sound to their advantage and created music with "dirt in it." To many, the gritty new sound made their music much more exciting. But most importantly, the British guys played old blues songs. They added their own "dirt" and re-imported the new sounds back to the States where they were originally produced. Already familiar with blues, Eyes and Strings immediately made the connection. For them, the *Invasion* fit their tastes in music perfectly; on the other hand, until told otherwise, Craze thought the songs were all originals.

The stage spectacles put the icing on the cake. The British had not only re-imported the blues, they copied how the blues guys acted on stage. Bands were no longer required to stand erect and wear uniforms. Individual performers could wear what they wanted and act like they wanted on stage. The combination of blues music and blues attitude allowed young new performers to "show their souls" on stage. The movement first dubbed themselves *The English Mod Cult,* and for *The Public Service,* especially Eyes and Craze, no more needed to be said. They were in hook, line and sinker.

The *British Invasion* did something else. By radically changing the musical tastes on the home front, things got much easier and more profitable for the blues artists here in the U.S. If not for the British, the blues might not have ever been introduced to "white America." The *Invasion* opened the doors of the "white" venues to the old blues artists, which in turn allowed young white audiences to hear the original blues entertainers for the first time.

B.B. King credited the English bands with introducing white America to their own black heritage. Craze once heard a story about the great *B.B. King* and the first time he played at *The Avalon Ball Room* in San Francisco. Up to that point, he and other black musicians had performed predominantly in front of black folks in black clubs. Never having played at the *Avalon* before, *B.B.* figured the ballroom was just another black club in San Francisco. As his bus turned the corner, he looked out his window and saw hundreds of young white people waiting in line outside the building. Taken by surprise, he thought maybe they had gone to the wrong place. After realizing the bus WAS in the right place, *B.B.* worried about how the young white crowd might respond to his show. Pleasantly, the receptive crowd welcomed his ice-breaking performance with open arms.

The British bands looked different from anything in music that had come before, and long hair became the most noticeable and important attribute of the *British Invasion* look. Many older people saw this exhibition as radical and feared it would lead to the "downfall of America's youth." In the fifties and early sixties, short haircuts called "crew cuts" and "flat tops" were the rage in America. The short-cut hairs were held up straight with a sticky substance called *Butch Wax*. When the recipient got too hot, the concoction melted, created a sticky mess, and oozed down the face and neck of the wearer.

Nobody wore their hair long in the early fifties in the States except "hoods," a term used at the time for supposed outlaws. They got their names because they wore their shirt collars up instead of folded down. The hoods had a different potion for holding their hair in place; they oiled their hair down with *Wild Root*. When Craze's dad did not have time to give Craze a haircut, he made Craze use the much more "civilized" and accepted *Vitalis Hair Tonic for Men*.

"I like *Wild Root* because it smells better. Every time I put *Vitalis* in my hair, I smell rubbing alcohol all day."

The British guys' hair looked natural and wild; so the greased-down hair look became obsolete.

In grade school, Lawder proudly donned the very sporty flat top, which made the top of his head look flat. Craze wore the much more practical crew cut, also a fashion statement in the fifties, which showed every irregularity in his skull. Lawder had a history of spending long hours on whatever hair-do he wore. He stood in front of a mirror until his hair had "just the right look." So during his flat top days, he made sure he used plenty of Butch Wax so the hair pointed straight up at all times. Craze did not use anything on his crew cut. But of course when his hair got too long, he used plenty of *Vitalis*. Even though he smelled like vodka, the tonic kept his wavy hair from sticking out in all the wrong places.

When the guys grew their hair long, Peter and Eyes lucked out in the hair department. Both were blessed with straight, dark brown hair, and their hair just fell in place like hair should do. Whether short or long, they looked well-groomed. Each could play an entire set without one hair falling out of place. Strings didn't care. He let his long, wavy hair "do whatever it wanted" and the messier his hair got, the better he looked. But Craze and Lawder had problems because they both had wavy-unmanageable hair. At gigs, they both started out looking presentable, but after a few songs their light brown, thin, wavy hair turned into sweaty messes, making them look like drowned rats. Craze and Lawder constantly searched for solutions to their hair problems.

When Lawder grew his hair long, he thought he had invented the process of "towel wrapping." After washing his hair, he used lots of his mom's hair spray and wrapped his still-wet hair in a towel, then waited for his hair to dry. While discussing their problem, Lawder said, "Craze it stays just where I want it...at least for a while." Craze knew Lawder had stretched the truth, but did not have the heart or nerve to call him on it.

Craze made the trek on his bike to Uptown Webster and the drug store located across the street from the record store where Eyes worked. As he pedaled the one-mile distance, Craze's mind focused on his mission: solving this nuisance once and for all. "They make all kinds of ladies hair stuff, so I'm sure I can find something that will take these stupid uncontrollable waves out of my hair. I just can't stand the front; it sticks straight out above my eyebrows and looks like I have a built-in baseball cap visor. Why couldn't I be born with straight hair like Eyes and Peter?"

Arriving at his destination, Craze executed his newly learned dismount; he jumped off his bike and let the two-wheeler slam into the brick wall and fall to the sidewalk. "Cool," he thought as he entered the front door. Making his way through the store, he read the signs above each aisle: "Let's see here, 'Pain and Headaches,' 'Dental Care,' 'Vitamins' …here we go, 'Shampoo and Hair Care.' Now we're in business."

"Let's see here, shampoo, hair coloring…here's something I've never heard of, 'hair relaxers.' He grabbed the white tube and read the ingredients.

"Lye, eggs, and potatoes, caution use sparingly…PERFECT, all natural." Craze had discovered the world of hair relaxers.

Arriving home with his new "miracle product" in the white tube, he thought, "Let's not waste any time. It's time to get to work."

He walked in the door and made his way up the steps and to the second-floor bathroom. Kneeling outside the tub like Lawder had taught him, Craze stuck his head under the faucet and soaked his hair. Not bothering with the directions, he squeezed the tube and filled his hand with the product. "It looks like toothpaste, but the smell kind of takes my breath away."

Trying to hold his breath as he rubbed the relaxer in his hair, he thought, "This stuff isn't foaming like shampoo; that don't look like enough. I guess I better use a little more. I'm sure that will make this stuff work even better. I think my hands are burning."

Craze continued lathering the toothpaste-looking product into his hair. "Now I'll just let it sit for three minutes."

After a few seconds, Craze noticed that the product now took his breath away and made his eyes burn terribly.

With his hands and head burning, after thirty seconds and gasping for air, Craze rinsed his hair, grabbed a towel and escaped to the fresh air of the hallway. Wheezing and half blind, he looked into the mirror in his room and through the tears running down his face, he tried focusing. Anxiously combing his hair, he peered into the mirror at his new straight hair-do. He thought, "Perfect!"

Then he noticed the hairbrush. "Man there's a lot of hair in that brush. Oh well, look how cool the hair left on my head looks. Success!"

After his hair dried, Craze returned to the now toxic-free bathroom and took another look in the mirror. "Maybe I used a little too much. I think those are burns on my forehead and the back of my neck; and I can't feel the tips of my fingers."

With his whole head now burning, Craze concluded, "Oh well, I'll just use a little less next time. That ought to solve the problem."

After a few more attempts, and using less and less relaxer, each time Craze ended with less and less hair and burnt to a crisp. His first reaction was, "Ah, it'll grow back in no time. Nobody will notice." But concerned about his future health, Craze finally gave up.

"Man I love the new 'do,' but I gotta quit. If I don't stop, I won't have any hair left, and I think I've lost some lung function."

Although Strings and Eyes both had charisma, each had their own distinctive look and completely different personalities. Their flamboyance and attitudes helped contribute to the unique personality of *The Public Service*. By observing Strings and Eyes in action, the other three guys in the band, Peter, Lawder, and Craze, learned how showmanship/stage presence worked. The three guys eagerly soaked up the other two guys' exploits on stage and devised their own versions of what they saw. The secret formula turned out to be: show YOUR SOUL and give it all to the audience.

From one of the guys, they also learned that you can go too far.

Although they both looked cool, Eyes and Strings dressed differently. Strings took the flamboyant approach of Jimi Hendrix.

His clothing defined the term *hippie* before the word came into existence. Craze later thought, "He dressed like Jimi Hendrix before there was a Jimi Hendrix."

Strings's tall, thin stature, along with shoulder-length curly brown hair, added to his persona. His dark facial features displayed a confidant *John Lennon*-like chiseled chin and nose. Strings usually decorated himself in tight, dirty blue jeans and a thin, white buttoned-down, puffy long-sleeved, collarless shirt. His brown leather vest always included at least one peace button. Strings accented his look with a feather tied in his hair and brightly colored scarves tied around his neck. Further, a turquoise bracelet and necklace, with more scarves hanging on his belt straps usually accompanied his decor. Sometimes his wardrobe included a brown leather cowboy hat with one side of the brim bent in an upright position. Since *Beatle Boots* were hard to come by, a pair of brown leather cowboy boots completed his fashion statement. He even smelled cool wearing Patchouli oil, a popular fragrance that smelled like pot. Even though not the greatest guitar player, for the most part, Strings made up for it with his coolness.

Sparked mostly by his interest in motorcycles, Eyes had a much simpler look. He browsed through motorcycle magazines and researched every bike. Ironically, the English bikes grabbed him the most. Craze thought, "He LOOKS like the English guys in those magazines, not the 'gang bikers' in the United States wearing their 'colors.'"

After saving enough money from the record store, and knowing that he could not afford his first choice, the American-made *Harley Davidson*, Eyes had narrowed his choices down to either a *Norton Atlas*, or a *Five Hundred Triumph*. In the meantime, he drove an old blue *Volkswagen* beetle with no brakes to save money.

"I'm getting close to having enough money, and I've got to make a decision. Besides, it's time to retire 'Old Blue' before I kill myself."

Eyes ended up purchasing a brand new *Five Hundred Triumph* motorcycle with a light-blue-and-silver tank.

Inspired by Eyes's new purchase, Craze thought, "Man, that bike's cool; one of these days I'm gonna get one."

Along with round horned-rimmed glasses, Eyes basically dressed in dark T- shirts, tight jeans, motorcycle boots sometimes and an occasional leather jacket. The look fit his tall thin frame, long legs, and straight long dark hair like a glove. His simpler appearance had just as much or even more effect than Strings's much more complicated peacock attire.

Strings had a unique way of getting people's attention. He acted like everybody owed him money. He fostered the illusion of importance through his outrageous self-promotion. He looked and acted-out the part of a rock star perfectly. No matter the location, Strings swaggered into any room, acting like he owned the joint.

Eyes had a completely different, but even more effective approach.

Craze mulled over these differences on more than one occasion. "What's the difference between their attitudes toward people in general? Strings draws everybody's attention by declaring through his actions, 'Look at me, look at me.' He forcefully takes over. He tells everybody that he's in charge. But after a while, people see through the bull. Eyes, on the other hand, makes everyone feel important. He's sincere; he genuinely cares and people sense it. On stage and in public, they want more of him and he gladly gives them what they want. He SHOWS them that he's in charge and people love it. But, I have to admit, when you combine the two personalities together, it has quite an effect on the audience."

The rest of the guys quickly figured out who really drove this bus of charisma, "and it wasn't Strings!"

"Guys, I've got an idea. On the B side of the *Satisfaction* record, there's a song called *'The Under-Assistant West Coast Promotion Man.'* It's a great song and nobody's ever heard of it. We can blow people's minds by playing such an obscure song and create our own version of the song; AND there's plenty more B-side songs out there to chose from."

So with Eyes's suggestion about playing unheard-of songs, and being minors, the recipe for success began for *The Public Service*. Eyes picked obscure songs from the British albums and with the help of the rest of the guys, they turned the songs into their own distinctive creations. It gave the band the cutting edge sound that they all desired—combined with Peter's musical training, Lawder's discipline, and Craze's unofficially elected leadership (more accurately booking agent, money handler, and anything else the rest of the guys did not want to do). Strings did add "coolness," so the rest of the guys put up with him acting like the boss. So the stage was set for the band to take on the world, or at least their hometown.

𝄞

Before rehearsal began, Craze gathered the troops.

"Hey man, I just got a great booking and I have an idea how to promote it. *Eden Seminary* is starting a teen-town, and they want us to be their first booking. They'll pay us a hundred and fifty bucks, so I booked the job. Besides that, the talent show at school is just a week before the gig, so we can use that show to promote the gig."

Well-rehearsed and prepared to take on the world, the guys set up for the talent show. Eyes had picked two songs written by British bands, *Talk, Talk* by *The Music Machine* and *My generation* by *The Who*. The band stood armed with their instruments and ready for the attack.

"Ladies and gentlemen, *The Public Service*."

CHAPTER 5

Before the curtain opened, Craze clicked off, "One, two, three, four," and started *Talk, Talk,* which created an air of mystery for the never-before-seen band. For the first time, *The Public Service* performed before a live audience. When the first song ended, the crowd started cheering, but the band did not pause. They broke into their final tune, *My Generation,* which stunned the audience. Finishing the song, the band immediately set their instruments down and left the stage while Eyes thanked the crowd and announced the upcoming gig at *Eden*. The band returned for their final bow as their new fans went wild.

𝄞

The band began their final preparations for the *Eden* gig. They planned how each set would start with a bang and end with an explosion. The recently successful rendition of *My Generation* would become the grand finale.

The final rehearsal in Craze's basement started as usual. As had become routine, neighborhood kids gathered outside the basement windows waiting to hear the music. Lawder, the self-appointed "dictator of rules," announced, "Get tuned; don't ruin the song just because you're too lazy to do the obvious." Lawder constantly insisted, "Don't ever play out of tune. If you're out of tune, stop playing and get in tune before you play another note. Playing in tune is easy; so, just do it."

But this time, things felt out of kilter. Weary from so many intense practices and the excitement of their first gig, the room seemed tense. On top of all the tension, Lawder's strings were worn out from so much rehearsal time. He said, "Sorry man, the music store was closed before I got there, so I couldn't pick up a new set of strings before practice. But I really did think that they'd last for one more practice."

Time after time, they started a tune and Lawder stopped the song to retune. Finally a string broke and Lawder shouted, "Stop, wait a minute. I have to try something."

The band nervously waited as Lawder tied two strings together in an effort to replace the broken one. Craze thought, "This ain't gonna work, and I'm worried about where it might lead. But I ain't gonna say anything."

The experiment did not go well and the guys sensed peril in the basement. They had witnessed Lawder's strength first hand, and, combined with his volcanic temper, they avoided the possibility of the two coming together at all costs. Craze thought, "We gotta do something, but what? We don't need a volcano in the basement; there's no escape path for me stuck here in the corner."

Terrified, Craze realized his very bad and dangerous predicament. He realized that he had set up his drums in the corner, between Lawder and the backdoor. As Lawder's ears and forehead turned as red as the Cardinal on a St. Louis jersey, Craze sensed the other guys plotting their escape route. Too "chicken" to say anything, they focused on Lawder's every move and obeyed his every command.

"Let's try it again." Lawder demanded as his string immediately went out of tune again. After several attempts and Lawder now glowing from anger, like an idiot, Craze foolishly rationalized in his mind, "Well, I AM the 'leader;' it's my job to do something."

"Maybe we should cancel rehearsal until you get new strings," he blurted out.

With the simple and ill-advised statement, Lawder reached his boiling point and the Volcano erupted.

The way Craze remembered it, the Volcano started with a low rumble. Lawder grabbed his fairly new, shiny-black *Hagstrum* bass guitar with one hand and the strings with the other. The strings went "plink, plink, plink, plink" as all four strings slowly gave way to his incredible strength and pulled away from the guitar. Momentarily forgetting the danger at hand, Craze thought, "What an amazing feat of strength and adrenaline. I've never seen that done before."

CHAPTER 5

Looking down at the ripped-off strings in his hand, Lawder threw them across the room, just missing Eyes's head (the only man standing). Now, staring blankly into space, and with his bass guitar still in on hand, Lawder whirled the guitar around like Pete Townsend of *The Who*. As batted equipment took flight, Craze thought, "This reminds me of the *Little Rascals* episode of 'The wild man of Borneo,' when Uncle George, the black sheep of the family, threw everybody out the window …Yum, yum, eat 'em up."

The other band members exited out the back door, leaving Craze to fend for himself. "Thanks guys," he thought.

While the Volcano and his Black *Hagstrum* mowed down mics, cymbals, amps, and other guitars, Craze somehow crawled past Lawder and out the back door to safety. A strange thought came to mind: "Wow, that was a sight to behold and I think I might to live to tell about it."

In the safety of the back yard, and not smart enough to escape like the neighborhood kids in the windows, the rest of the band gathered like puppies waiting to be devoured by the oncoming lava flow.

After a period of time, the turmoil settled down in the basement. The guys waited with baited breath as they sensed the monster-lava leaving the cave, prepared to run if necessary. Lawder exited the basement door into the cool night air. With the volcano's redness gone, the eruption ended. Lawder meekly smoldered, "Sorry guys, I guess we'll have to wait until I get new strings."

Craze thought, "I think I saw smoke coming out of his mouth."

Lawder calmly walked into the sunset, got in his car and drove away. Re-entering the scene of the crime, the band surveyed the damage. To their amazement, minimal damage had resulted except for Lawder's bass. The guitar now sported a sizable chuck of shiny black paint missing out of its side.

"Lawder ain't gonna like that one bit!" Craze said.

The "Old English" style campus of *Eden Seminary* sat across the street and down the block from the guys' high school. The tower in the middle of the campus duplicated the one located at Oxford in England. The room selected for the teen-town had the same "Old English" architecture as the rest of the campus. As Craze and Eyes entered the room, the large-enough-to-walk-into fireplace located at one end grabbed their attention.

Eyes said, "Wouldn't it be cool to set up in that fireplace? The whole room focuses on that spot. It's the perfect location for a stage, so let's just make the fireplace into the stage."

Having set up earlier in the day, the guys met at Craze's house and prepared for their attack on *Eden*. Led by Eyes on his new motorcycle, the rest of the guys followed in Peter's newly acquired Volkswagen van. As they approached the venue, each member sat in silence, like a football team anticipating the start of a big game. Craze thought, "Well, everything's done but the playing."

Eyes entered the parking lot first, followed by Peter's new van. Blown away by the large crowd waiting to get in, Craze thought, "It worked! The talent show drew a big crowd…cool man."

Dressed in their coolest clothes, the band pushed their way through the crowd and to the fireplace stage. Lawder surprised the guys in the band when he reached behind his amp and pulled out a serape and a huge Mexican sombrero. He then sat in front of his amp for the entire gig completely covered by the serape and sombrero with only the neck of his bass sticking out. From time to time, Craze heard members of the crowd saying things like, "Hey Lawder, what you doin' under there?" and "Man, he's weird; he must be on drugs."

Catching wind of the comments, Eyes announced over the microphone, "People please don't bother the bass player; he's meditating. If disturbed at the improper moment, he might enter the wrong chakra and that would be unpleasant for all."

Lawder even stayed under the serape and sombrero during the breaks. During one break, and trying not to draw attention, Craze quietly moseyed over to Lawder's side and asked, "Hey Lawder, you okay under there? Can I get you a Coke or something?"

Lawder slowly raised his head high enough for Craze to see one eyeball and the smile on his face. "No I'm fine; I'm having a ball. As long as I can see Eyes from under this hat, I'm good. Go away before you ruin the effect."

Craze shrugged his shoulders and obediently walked away, thinking, "Only Lawder ..."

Following Eyes's lead, the evening went on as the guys successfully executed their planned attack on the sold-out audience. Craze, who had actually set up inside the fireplace behind the rest of the guys, thought, "What a cool vantage point; I never thought that I'd actually play inside a real fireplace. Everything's working, and Eyes is like a people magnet. He's admired by everybody. I won't forget this night."

Earlier in the week, Craze had painfully made out the order of songs for each set, which the band appropriately called "the list." At his house before the gig, he gave each member a copy. When Eyes got his copy, he half jokingly replied, "Craze, you really expect me to read these chicken scratchins?" (Which, by the way, from that gig on, Eyes said to Craze every time he got handed 'the list.') "By the way, take *Train Kept a Rollin'* out of the last set."

Confused, Craze asked, "Why, it's one of our best songs?"

Eyes replied with one word: "Encore!"

"Oh, okay."

Eyes turned around to the band and announced, "Last song, *My Generation*; Craze count it off…"

The Public Service ended their final set, and left the stage, leaving only the red lights of their amps behind. The crowd went wild demanding an encore.

Eyes turned to Craze and said, "Told you…Guys follow me; we're gonna kill them with *Train Kept a Rollin.*'"

The band headed back to the fireplace and ended the night. This time with sombrero and serape removed, Lawder took his rightful position next to the rest of the band. After doing their *Yardbirds* rendition of *Train Kept a Rollin'*, the band walked off stage, joined the crowd, and thanked them for their wonderful reception.

𝄞

Over the next several months, the band did extremely well gigging in the area. They made enough money for Eyes to buy new microphones and stands and a new royal-blue-colored, "rolled and pleated" *Kustom P.A.* system. To get a better "high-end" sound, Eyes added old-style horn speakers on top of each speaker cabinet. He then painted the horns yellow and black, which resembled the back-ends of bees.

Eventually Craze bought a *Ludwig* drum kit with a Ringo Starr-like oyster-pearl gray finish from a guy named Billy. (Later on, Billy would play an important part in all of the guys' lives.) Craze also bought a *Honda 250 Scrambler* joining Eyes in the world of motorcycles.

After the abnormal death of his prized *Hagstrum* bass guitar, Lawder bought a *Fender Bassman* bass guitar. He also purchased a huge *Epiphone* amp.

Peter spent the most money by purchasing a white *Fender Mustang* guitar, a sunburst-colored *Fender Telecaster* and a *Fender*

Bassman amp. His last, most expensive, and most important purchase, an *M2 Hammond* organ with *Leslie* speakers, finally allowed him to play his God-given instrument: a keyboard. The *Hammond* opened doors to music previously unobtainable to the band and significantly increased their musical possibilities.

Now equipped for any situation, Craze couldn't wait to fill the guys in on his latest booking.

Chapter 6

God's Gifted

Craze patiently waited for the right moment so that he could get maximum impact out of his announcement. But before he could say anything, as usual, Strings blasted into rehearsal and immediately took over. The band let him think of himself as the boss because "it was just easier that way." Strings ranted on about how well one of his ideas worked on a song that they had played for the first time at their last gig and went on saying something about the band paying more attention to him in the future.

After a short time, Eyes interrupted, "Hey man, I think Craze has something to say. Go ahead Craze, I've been waiting to hear the news that you mentioned to me yesterday."

Craze stood up from behind his drum set and began, "Well guys first of all I found out that the Allman brothers changed their name from *The Allman Joy* to *The Hour Glass*. All I know is that it had something to do with their move to L.A. You can ask them about it yourselves when we PLAY WITH THEM IN THREE WEEKS. I just booked the gig at *The Castaways* (a local hot spot), and I've been busting at the seams to tell you guys the good news."

Thrilled by the news, the band responded in unison, "Cool man."

Figure 9. Castaway's business card.

Craze thought back about how this whole Allman brothers' thing had started: At rehearsal one night, Strings gave his usual orders: "Friday night we're off, so we're all going to check out this new band. You won't believe these guys."

He continued, "They're called *The Allman Joy* and man, these dudes are fantastic. Wait 'til you get a load of the guitar player and his brother on a *B3 Hammond*."

Instead of arguing, as each guy thought about canceling their individual plans for this rare weekend night off, Eyes spoke up, "You know guys, this plan could go under the category of business, and Strings IS usually right about these things, so I'm in… I suggest that we take a vote."

So they took a vote, and following Eyes's lead, the band agreed with the plan.

Located in the basement of a parking garage located in the heart of the city, the band entered a dimly lit establishment. Along with the lights behind the bar, a small mirror ball inserted in the headless bass drum and ignited by a tiny spotlight provided the only illumination in the flat-black painted club. The rotating ball attached to the top of the drum acted like a cannon in the bass drum, shooting beams of light all over the club. The shafts of mirror-ball light blinded the few gathering fans from observing the activities on stage. Only fifteen people occupied the club, and *The Public Service* accounted for five of those occupants. Craze thought, as he prepared to go home disappointed, "Usually with such a small crowd, a band will play crappy."

Craze squinted, trying to observe the movements on the bandstand. Although he could not see the inhabitants very well, what he COULD see alarmed him. He thought, "Wait a minute, all the bottom drum heads are missing. You can't remove those heads. The drums won't sound right."

Getting excited, he also detected two keyboards, an electric piano, and a *B-3 Hammond Organ*. "Two keyboards - nobody has two keyboards and who is going to play all those guitars sitting on stands? Mirror balls, no drum heads, and two keyboards… what's going on?"

All of a sudden, POW, all the instruments came to life, blasting magnificent sounds. At the same instant, the stage exploded with light. Up front, mid-stage stood Duane Allman, wailing lead guitar parts on his *Les Paul Gibson*, while his brother, Gregg Allman, singing in his deep, raspy voice, sat stage left behind his *Hammond Organ*. Alongside the two brothers, Paul Hornsby sat playing a second keyboard while Jess Willard stood stage right playing bass guitar. Johnny Sandlin, the drummer, sat behind his headless drums in the back. Craze felt like a "St. Louis tornado" had just ripped through the building. Duane attacked the words,

> Don't want you no more,
> Don't want you no more,
> Don't want your loving baby,
> Don't want you no more . . .

This *Allman Joy* band created sounds that Craze and the rest of the guys in this band had never encountered before. Awe-inspired by this abrupt beginning, Craze thought, "These two guys and their band are burning the place down and with two keyboards to boot. The brothers are playing exactly the same notes. Hell, the whole band is playing the exact-same notes."

Eyes leaned over to Craze and said, "Powerful stuff…"

The five guys in the small audience had never encountered such musical muscle. Craze thought, "So much for being disappointed; it's obvious that a small crowd ain't gonna affect these guys' attitude. They're on a musical mission!" *The Public Service* had just gotten their first taste of Duane and Gregg Allman's genius.

With no hesitation, *Allman Joy* burst into their second song, a complete departure from the first. They displayed their exquisite use of dynamics in an old blues number by *Bessie Smith*, "Nobody Loves You When You're Down and Out," which almost topped their initial offering. Craze thought, "It's amazing how they put their personalities into those arrangements; most importantly, I feel them playing these songs FOR the audience, not for themselves. I can literally feel their soul."

Skillfully attacking each song with pinpoint precision, the evening went on as *Allman Joy* rapid-fired song after song. Later in the evening, their skillful use of dynamics also enhanced the song made famous by *Otis Redding*, "Try a Little Tenderness." Craze took further notes. "Some of their originals are very cool. The slowing-down of the ending on 'To Things Before' rocked."

Lawder agreed; he liked the bass line in "I Still Want Your Love," while Peter especially enjoyed the unconventional chord changes in "Going Nowhere." For the first time, the guys witnessed greatness, "up close and personal." The remarkable beginnings, the dynamic middles, and stunning endings of all their songs kept the audience begging for more. *The Public Service* had never heard rock music played so brilliantly.

Craze thought, "They just stand up there and reveal their souls. They're as comfortable on stage as they would be sitting on their couch at home. This show is the definition of real professionalism."

After the gig, *The Public Service* stuck around and met their new heroes.

🎼

Driving home in Peter's van, and feeling that their lives had somehow changed, Strings spoke first: "Man I told you guys they were great. You need to listen to me more often. I've got plenty of new ideas for the band, and you guys have got to pay more attention to my ideas."

A little annoyed by Strings's comments, Craze spoke next. "Man can you guys believe those guys; two keyboards…nobody does that? And when the keyboard player picked up his guitar and joined Duane on those dual leads I freaked out. Here's what really got me. The size of the crowd didn't matter to these guys. They played like 10,000 people were there. By the way, I wonder where the drummer came up with the no drumhead idea. I thought it would make the drums sound crappy."

Eyes spoke next: "The instruments harmonizing on top of the vocals blew my mind. We gotta do that. And we can learn from their show. We need stage presence like that. Little things like Duane's face added a lot. You could see his soul in his face."

As he drove down the road, Peter began, "Guys, we can do better. We need to get to work. These guys are the perfect models. What they do with their songs blows my mind. We can do that. Most of this stuff is within our reach. Think about how cool it would be to add this stuff to our way of doing things."

The Public Service considered themselves lucky because of the small crowd; they felt as if they received their own exclusive concert from the *Allman Joy*. They knew they had witnessed the beginning of something really big and a new way of doing things in rock music. The Allman brothers and their band did not care about the size of the crowd; they played their hearts out anyway. Simply put, *The Public Service* just witnessed the greatest musical performance they had ever seen and sensed history unfolding before their eyes.

The Public Service learned a lot that night. For the first time, Craze's band heard the brothers play their patented dual harmonized guitar solos, which later elevated them to superstardom. They also witnessed their powerful use of multiple instrumental harmonies following the melody line. No other band in the history of rock had ever used these two weapons so effectively.

Eyes sized up the situation for everybody, adding, "We want to compete on a higher level and the Allman brothers just provided the ingredients. They furnished us with a whole new understanding of what it takes to be a professional band. We already have a fine work ethic, so now we have the ammunition to overhaul every aspect of the band. We can use this opportunity to move up a notch in the rock world."

Lawder spoke last, "Yeah and I'm gonna make sure we do it right..."

In the days to come, and obsessed by what he had heard, Craze spent hours thinking about *Allman Joy*: "What exactly separates them from anybody else that we've ever heard? I guess because the show felt so natural and unrehearsed. It's like they're 'seasoned.' It's obvious that they've rehearsed every aspect of this show so much and done this whole thing so many times that they no longer have to worry about WHAT they're doing. Their muscle memory takes over and THAT'S THEIR SECRET: repetition and attention to detail. Now they can SHOW the crowd how much they love and believe in what they're doing.

"And here's the real kicker; their performance isn't even the best thing about this band. All these guys are outstanding musicians, but Duane is by far the best musician that I've ever heard. This guy was born with guitar playing in his blood. It's like he and his guitar are one; his guitar is an extension of his body. He IS his instrument. Gregg's voice and keyboard playing is really good, but Duane is the real captain of this ship. Man, can he play!"

𝄞

Duane Allman purchased his first guitar in 1960 at Sears Roebuck for $21.95. That purchase planted the seed for what grew into one of the most supreme guitar players of all time. On stage Duane and his guitar created a larger-than-life image of quiet charisma. His seasoned self-confidence and understated bodily expressions assaulted his audience with devastating guitar licks. His facial expressions and quiet dominance offered a gateway to his soul. He simply mesmerized his audiences into submission.

𝄞

The night of the *Castaway* gig, the two bands got re-acquainted. As *The Public Service* set up for their performance, the guys in *The Hour Glass*, formerly the *Allman Joy*, entered the building. They walked up to the stage, and the two bands talked among themselves.

Eyes said, "Hey man, I read about your new name. What's up with that?"

"Yeah man, the last time we were here we met a guy who wanted to promote us; so we moved to L.A. and changed our name to *The Hour Glass*," Duane answered.

"Cool how'd that go?" Eyes responded.

Duane replied, "I don't know man, we made two albums but we weren't too happy with the direction this guy took us so we got out of there. Now we have these records to sell so we don't lose a bunch of money. We're doing a record release thing tomorrow at this record store in town. Why don't you guys show up?"

With the rest of the guys nodding their heads in approval, Eyes responded, "Cool man, we'll be there; it sounds like a blast."

The Public Service played their set with Eyes mentioning their heroes-with-the new-name, *The Hour Glass,* several times during the performance. After doing their job as the opening band, *The Public Service* cleared the stage and prepared for the upcoming treat.

Besides doing many of their familiar blues covers, the Allman brothers introduced new original songs from their albums like "Power of Love" and "Changing of the Guard." Led by Duane's stunning slide guitar solos and Gregg's outstanding gravelly voice and heavy-handed *B3 Hammond,* breathtaking music filled the room, blowing the crowd's mind.

Craze thought, "These guys are too much; they're killing this audience just like they killed us a few weeks ago. I've never been so happy getting slaughtered by another band on stage."

Though not from St. Louis, they sent their new St. Louis audience home feeling like something special had just happened in their lives…and it had. Loading up after the gig, Gregg walked over to *The Public Service* and asked, "Hey man, we're having a party. Would you guys like to come? If you want to go, you can follow us over to our hotel."

Familiar with the sleazy neighborhood and run-down hotel from a past bad experience, the guys did not hesitate. "Sure," they responded in unison. Now they had two events planned with their new friends, the Allman brothers.

While loading, Craze thought about the gig, "What a sight to behold man; Duane and Eyes performing back-to-back on the same stage; that was cool. Two of the most charismatic people I know on the same stage. They've both got 'IT,' this charisma thing, down to a science. It's all about a natural-born confidence—nothing cocky at all. You know, I'm lucky to have a best friend with 'IT.' I think about it this way: I'm watching this *Lone Ranger* from my perspective as his sidekick, *Tonto.* And nobody else will ever know what a 'hoot' it is being Eyes's *Tonto.*"

𝄞

Craze had thought about this charisma thing many times before. "Everybody's seen this 'It' thing in popular public figures like *Frank Sinatra* or *Elvis*. They just never had a front row seat like I do. What makes people stop what they're doing and gaze at them? I have no idea. Somehow their body confidence says, 'Here I am and you'll never forget me.'

"What makes him tick? It never fails. All Eyes has to do is enter a room and everybody turns and looks at him; he's like a light switch. 'IT' doesn't just happen on stage; he always has that air about him every time he's around people. He doesn't have to do anything special; he just walks into a room and the whole place lights up. His star power follows him around like a little dog.

"When Eyes gets in the room, people flock to him, vying for his attention and he happily obliges. They love it. He makes everyone feel like his close personal friend. To top it off, he remembers everything anybody ever told him. Then he seals the deal by asking questions about their last conversations. How does he remember all that stuff? Finally, a remarkable thing happens; his fans start COPYING HIS MANNERISMS …amazing."

"I thought it was a dream . . .?"

Then Craze thought, "This questionable dream has bugged me for years. I think it was a dream, but I'm not sure. Then I think my brain just took a bunch of experiences and combined them all together. But why does this dream bug me so much? Why does it matter at all? Of all the things that happened to our band, why does this particular event haunt me so much?"

This "uncertain dream" in Craze's head went like this: *The Public Service* and *The Hour Glass* went to a party and the two bands entered an old, broken-down hotel together. The *Lone*

Rangers, the leaders...no masks of course, Duane and Eyes lead the way followed by their sidekicks, the *Tontos*, Greg and Craze. The rest of the band members followed behind them. Climbing steps to the third floor, they heard the rumble of guests' voices coming out of already-packed large rooms upstairs. Reaching the third floor landing, Craze unconsciously prepared himself for the usual "Eyes's reception," when the people in the room turned and looked at him. But this time Craze witnessed something profound. As the two *Lone Rangers* entered the room, everybody in the room stopped, turned, and looked at...DUANE.

As the dream continued, Craze thought, "This is a first, man. Duane just beat Eyes at his own game, and I'm the only one who noticed. This guy has REALLY GOT IT."

One morning many years later, Craze woke up and opened his eyes, thinking, "That's it! My reference point for charismatic personalities was Eyes, and this dream defined the absolute supremacy of Duane's personality. Eyes couldn't hold a candle to Duane's charisma. We knew in our hearts that Duane was a superstar; the world just didn't know it yet. We were there; we watched the birth of a star and his band. How many people can say that they ever had an experience like that? IT WAS AN OMEN!"

No longer "haunted" by the dream and in his sixties, Craze talked to his old friend Peter. During the conversation and out of the clear blue, Peter stated, "Hey you remember the time we went to that sleazy hotel with the Allman brothers, and everybody looked at Duane?"

Note to Craze..."It really wasn't a dream!"

𝄞

Ready to hang out with their heroes, *The Hour Glass*, and their adoring fans, *The Public Service* anxiously entered the store. But what they saw in the record store told a completely different story. A few customers mulled through the record racks, while the Allman brothers stood in the back of the store all by themselves. *The Public Service* made their way to the back of the store. One of the brothers spoke up, "Hey man thanks for showing up. This is bad, man; we needed some company."

Their relative obscurity and zero promotions, except for the "word of mouth" plugs at last night's gig, created a difficult time for their out-of-town friends. With nobody else there the two bands used this occasion to get better acquainted.

Craze went home anxiously anticipating the new albums. After listening to both albums, Craze thought, "I'm really happy to have two records by these guys, but whoever recorded this thing really missed the boat. These two albums don't sound anything like *The Hour Glass* sounds live. The second album is better than the first because it contains originals. But now I know what Duane was talking about when he mentioned to Eyes their 'problematic' experience in L.A. Something else is gonna to have to happen to put these guys over the top."

Lawder took his self-assigned seat behind the driver, Craze, in Craze's parents' sixty-two *Chevy station wagon*. Craze thought back to the day when that seat became Lawder's. Peter had climbed in the back seat first, when Lawder walked over to the door and demanded, "Hey, scoot over; you're in my seat."

With the look of "that really makes me mad" on his face, Peter grudgingly moved over to the worst seat in the car, middle of the back seat. Luckily for Strings, he had already climbed in the other back-window seat. Peter complained, "The hump in the middle of this seat is really uncomfortable."

Eyes replied from his comfortable front passenger seat, "Oh, that's a shame; who votes for making this seating arrangement permanent? All in favor raise your hand."

Everybody but Peter raised his hand in favor. So from then on, Lawder sat directly behind the driver, and Peter sat on the hump. Craze later thought, "Maybe that's why Peter shelled out all that money for his van so early in the game."

After a gig one night, Lawder sat in "his" back seat and spoke up: "Hey man, I'm starving; let's eat."

Hungry himself, Craze drove the band-member-filled, equipment-laden *Chevy* to a local drive-in hamburger joint. While everybody in the car innocently minded their own business and wolfed down burgers and fries, suddenly a load of "St. Louis Greasers" ("rednecks" in today's language) pulled in a slot across the parking lot, in a '49 black *Mercury*. As "St. Louis Greasers" did back then, they began heckling the guys in the *Chevy* about their long hair and funny-looking clothing. At the time, longhairs faced danger in certain neighborhoods in the city. "Rednecks," also known as "Hoosiers" in St. Louis, did not take to the new fashion statements kindly. Beating up "these guys who look like girls" became their sport. Later on in the eighties, these same "Hoosiers" brought the mullet into style.

Leaning out the windows of the *'49 Merc,* they made the usual ignorant comments like: "You look like a bunch of girls" and "Do you guys use Revlon products?"

Making sure that the whole parking lot took notice of their existence, the "rednecks" kept up their steady barrage against the band's manhood.

Being in the front seat, Craze worried because he could not see Lawder's face. Slowly turning his eyes, and making sure not to catch Lawder's attention, Craze scoped out the expressions on Eyes's and Strings's faces and thought, "I guess everything's okay; the other the guys in the car don't look worried. Apparently, Lawder's ignoring the rhubarb going on outside."

Unknown to Craze, the Volcano WAS glowing back there. Completely taken by surprise by the occupants of the car, the Volcano erupted. The eruption started with the back door swinging open, allowing a magma flow out of its opening. Glowing red from top to bottom, Lawder surged out of the back seat and opened the tailgate of the station wagon. The magma swelled over the tailgate and consumed Craze's 20-inch *Zyljian cymbal*. The Volcano rose up in all its magnificence, flailing the cymbal like a giant brass saw blade. As the cymbal-bladed Volcano flowed across the parking lot toward the *Black Mercury*, the Volcano belched in a deep, bloodcurdling voice, "I'm going to cut your f$#!^%# heads off."

Before the sharp-edged Volcano slashed the "Hoosier" occupants to pieces, they rolled their windows up, locked their doors and escaped, leaving the perilous Volcano spewing in the parking lot. Mercifully, the "chickens" in the black car avoided death and mutilation. Watching the taillights speeding away from the burger joint, the Volcano cooled and lost its redness. Lawder calmly put the cymbal back in the car, got back into the back seat, and finished eating. Nobody said a word.

Craze thought, "Wow, with the name *Velvet Underground*, I bet this place is cool. There's a place in California using that same name; I guess they built a new club here. I'm not sure why they'd spend money in that particular location, but stranger things have happened. Maybe they're restoring all those old bars located in that worn-out three-block area? I usually don't take gigs that only offer the 'cover charge' for pay, but we're popular enough; I'm sure we'll make a bunch of dough."

So Craze rationalized his way into accepting the gig, located in a "bad section" of the inner city. The neighborhoods got worse the closer they got to the club. Checking the address, and realizing that nobody had done a thing to the neighborhood, Craze thought, "This can't be right, this is an old boarded-up brick house; it's not even one of the clubs."

CHAPTER 6

Located at the end of the three-block stretch of old dilapidated bars stood the graffiti-covered structure with plywood-covered windows. On the side of the building, Craze noticed a sloppily hand painted wooden sign with purple letters, reading *Velvet Underground,* and an arrow pointing down to the basement steps.

"This must be it," Craze thought. "Man, they took the 'Underground' thing literally. This place is a rat-trap. I hope the vibrations of the music don't bring the whole building down. This is scary; I'm not sure I even want to get out of the car."

As the band walked down the broken steps and entered the damp basement, they took in its horrifying interior. Ducking the low-hanging, drippy pipes as they entered, they saw a wooden-looking box-thing on one side of the basement that the owners called "the bar" and a few tables and chairs scattered around the floor. One of the proprietors spoke up, "Isn't this cool, man? Just feel the vibes. By the way, set up over there in that dark spot where we've cleared a spot."

With the owner pointing to the wall opposite the low-hanging door, Eyes said to Craze, "Craze, what have you done?"

Craze set up his drums while he listened to the grumbles coming out of the rest of the guys. He thought, "Man, am I gonna hear about this later; I screwed this one up big time. This place sure isn't the shiny new club I had pictured. These owner-guys are full of crap. This place is more like a toxic-waste dump…I think I'm having an asthma attack breathing this air."

Only six shady characters showed as the audience. But as taught by their heroes, the band dutifully fulfilled their obligation and played their best in the contaminated environment. Craze found out later that most of THEIR own fans did not show up because their parents would not allow them go to such a bad neighborhood.

At the end of the gig, the owner walked over and handed Craze six dollars. Eyes responded, "Well, at least we know he ain't lyin'; he gave us all the door money."

Eyes continued while the rest of the band stood behind him: "Six dollars, we made six dollars? What were you thinking, are you nuts? Craze, it's gonna be a long time for you to live this one down."

Licking his well-deserved wounds, Craze finished packing. As the band loaded the van, an old beat-up car passed by full of unsavory characters staring at their equipment. Craze thought as he loaded his bass drum, "I hope we don't get robbed or something worse. This place might not be the best place to leave our equipment alone in the middle of night. I better stand guard out here with the van, while the rest of the guys haul the equipment."

To his relief, Craze noticed the mood of the guys changing. They started laughing about the gig. Lawder spoke up with humor in his voice, "Well that sucked; this one is hard to believe."

Lawder stopped his chat and pointed down the street to two guys walking down the street towards them. Lawder said, "Hey look you guys, isn't that Duane and Gregg Allman?"

As the two approached, Gregg spoke up first: "Hey man, we heard you guys were playing down here. We just finished playing a gig down the street and we're staying at hotel down here. We thought we'd come by and say hi. I guess we're too late to hear you guys. Man, we took a beating tonight; we only made four bucks apiece. How did you guys do?"

Craze laughed and said, "Well, you did better than we did. The whole band only made six bucks."

The group finished their conversation and the Allman brothers headed back in the same direction to their sleazy hotel. The guys piled in the van and drove off. Eyes spoke up, "Craze, you just got lucky, this whole debacle ended on a good note. If these guys ever make it big, and they will…we'll have something to tell our grandkids."

CHAPTER 6

Also known as *Skydog*, Duane Allman's reputation as an elite guitar player skyrocketed, and many polls at that time rated him as one of the top five elite guitar players in the world. On October 29, 1971, Duane Allman died in a motorcycle crash in Macon, Georgia.

𝄞

With the band armed with new equipment, the question became: "How do we get the best 'bang for our buck'?"

The Public Service knew that their sound had drastically improved and that the *Hammond* opened a whole new world of possibilities, musically, but what about visually?

"What could we do visually besides bee-horns on top of the speakers?" Peter came up with an idea: "Eyes, I've got an idea. You know the song on *The Hour Glass* album, 'To Things Before'? Well, guess what; there's only one note played on the *Hammond* throughout the whole song. You have to kick on the *Leslie* speaker every once in a while, and work the volume pedal, but that's no problem. I think YOU should play keyboard on that song. Just think about it, we could make a big 'to do' about it on stage, 'and now making his instrumental debut on the *Hammond* organ, the one and only Eyes'...or something like that."

Craze joined in, "Yeah man, we could have our own 'Gregg' on stage!"

Eyes skeptically replied, "Well, I guess so; let me think about it."

"Great idea; let's take a vote," Lawder said.

Eyes said, "Wait, wait, wait, I said that I wanted to think about it."

Lawder responded, "You've had plenty of time to think about it, and if we give you any more time, you'll think of a reason to say 'no.' So now is as good a time as any to take a vote."

So with a vote of four yes and one abstention, because of

"confusion," Eyes learned what note to push, how to adjust the volume, and when to turn the *Leslie* on and off.

On the night of Eyes's big instrumental debut, the big moment arrived. He leaned to the guys, "Let's play this one down; I think we'll get a better reception."

With no fanfare, Peter got up from the *Hammond* and put on his guitar. In the meantime, Eyes left his spot in front of the band and sat behind the keyboard. Caught by surprise, people who knew the band wondered, "What's going on?" Craze counted off the song. Eyes successfully completed his task by perfectly pushing his one note, operating the *Leslie*, and working the volume pedal while singing the song. As usual, Eyes played his part to the hilt, moving around in his seat, like he was really doing something.

After the song, Eyes and Peter returned to their usual positions, and for effect acted like nothing unusual had just happened. As Eyes returned to his original position, the crowd went nuts! He calmly said, "Thank you everybody, thank you . . . our next song will be..." as if nothing special had just happened.

"Man, this guy really knows what he's doing," Craze thought.

𝄞

The Public Service had front row seats witnessing the early development of *The Allman Brothers* and their climb to super stardom. *The Public Service* also had the unique position of learning from the best what it meant to be a professional band. Thanks to *The Allman Brothers*, *The Public Service* made themselves into a better band.

The most important lessons: "Respect all audiences, no matter what size, and always give your best effort, because, in the end, they will be your judge."

Only one question remained for the guys: "Who's going to replace Strings?"

Chapter 7

Black Sheep Bird

After a year and a half in the band, Strings's time in *The Public Service* came to an end. Strings, being the oldest, graduated first and departed for college. The band put out the word that they needed a lead guitar player, and tryouts began in Craze's basement. As tryouts began, Craze thought, "We've all known each other for so many years; it's gonna be weird having an 'outsider' join our tight group. On the other hand, it is kind of exciting."

Not long after tryouts began, a quiet skinny, little guy with dark long hair entered the room. Craze thought, "I've got to say he looks like a lead guitar player."

The kid opened his guitar case and pulled out an extremely rare, left-handed *Fender Stratocaster*. The left-handed guitar playing kid spoke: "Hi, I'm Bird or you can call me Birdman."

Without saying anything else, he plugged in his guitar and tuned up. Lawder muttered, "Good start."

Bird wailed several loud, complicated riffs on his *Strat*. As he quietly continued playing intricate riffs on his guitar, he looked up. "Ready."

Peter spoke up, "Well let's get started. Tell us a little about your family; where you live?"

Still piddling around on his guitar and not looking up, Bird responded, "I live in Brentwood and my dad's a 'shrink.'"

Satisfied with his answer, Peter continued, "What kind of music do you like?"

"Oh I don't know, I guess the blues. I've heard you guys a lot and I like the stuff you do."

Next question: "Well are you prepared to make all rehearsals and band jobs? You know, we're very busy."

Bird, still fiddling on his guitar, answered, "Sure man, no problem."

Getting antsy, Eyes spoke up next: "Well let's cut to the chase, you know '*Train Kept a Rollin*'?"

"Yeah, wanna play it?" the kid responded.

Before Eyes could reply, and catching everybody by surprise, Bird stood up and blasted out the lead intro to the song. The guys quickly jumped into action following his lead. Birdman skillfully executed his part through the whole song. Finishing the song, Bird sat back down and continued his fiddling. Eyes spoke up again.

"Okay man, here's what we're gonna do. I'll call off the songs and you follow. If you don't know the song, stop me and we'll go over it with you."

Not looking up, Bird replied, "No problem, I know all your stuff."

Song after song, a confident Birdman flawlessly performed his parts, looking great while he did them. After several numbers, Lawder halted the proceedings and stated, "Okay, great, we'll get a hold of you."

Bird responded, "Okay, thanks."

Saying nothing else, Birdman packed up his gear and left the basement, leaving the guys behind thinking about what had just happened. Eyes spoke up first. "He's a little mental, but I like mental; mental is kind of cool. After all, his dad IS a shrink. Anyway, he sure knows his stuff."

Craze added his two cents. "Man, the kid can play. I think

he'll look real good on stage. But did you notice he never made eye contact with us except for signals?"

Peter's turn next: "We certainly won't have to spend much rehearsal time. He already knows our stuff. I just hope he knows what he's in for with our schedule and everything."

Finally Lawder spoke up. "I can crap bigger than that little turd, but the kid is a really good guitar player and like Craze says, he looks the part. He just better not mess around on his guitar like that during rehearsals or at jobs."

Eyes said, "We have to remember that it's gonna take time for us to get used to this change…well, let's take a vote."

So the four voted unanimously, and Birdman became the new lead guitar player and youngest member of *The Public Service*.

With Strings gone and Bird at lead guitar, a new era began in the band. Craze thought, "Rehearsals feel completely different; it's as different as day and night. But at this point, I'm not sure if Bird is the day, or the night. Strings acted like the boss; Bird doesn't care, he doesn't have opinions and he's got only one answer for everything, 'I don't care, just tell me when it's my turn.' The only thing he cares about in life is that *Strat*…well and girls too."

The guys worried about Bird, or any body else for that matter, handling such strict rules. So to some extent, they knew that their way of doing things would take some getting used to. Bird always showed up on time, ready for jobs and rehearsals or anything else required. But as Craze put it, "He's here in body, but I'm not sure about his mind. Don't get me wrong, he gives a hundred percent, but paying attention isn't his strong point. I think he's listening, but I'm not sure. Obviously, his mind is lost in that guitar and that's not all bad. But it sure is irritating sometimes."

Lines like, "Hey man, are you paying attention?" or "Quit farting around" or "Turn down" or especially "Knock it off" became part of the band's lingo after Bird joined the band. Birdman just could not stop himself; he HAD to wail on that *Strat*. Out of the blue, he would rip into a lead part that had nothing to do with what was going on. Seemingly not paying attention, head buried, fiddling around on his guitar became one of his most irritating habits. When not goofing around, Bird played great and looked great on stage. He became an asset to the band.

Craze thought, "This kid is like a fish taking to water when he gets on stage; he's a wild man. Looking good doesn't hurt either; the girls flock to him. He may not be in Eyes' league, but not many are for that matter."

Because of Bird's good looks and outstanding stage presence, many girls fell in "love" with him, which turned into a big problem. He loved the ladies back. A particularly horny little dude, Bird could not resist the temptation. Unlike the other guys in the band who had learned there's a time and a place for everything; "take care of business first then go play with the girls."

When it came to girls, Bird completely lost control. On stage, he behaved himself most of the time. But the rest of the time, during breaks and at the end of shows, Bird had real problems. He would just disappear…MIA.

After breaks, Bird always returned to the stage late while the rest of the band stood waiting on stage, ready for the next set. Bird usually came sashaying back with a girl on his arm, lipstick on his face, and a big stupid grin. He looked like a guilty fox with a feather sticking out of his mouth.

The biggest sins came at the end of gigs. "The call of the Sirens" proved too much for Bird's system. By that time of night, with everybody exhausted, tearing down and loading equipment, it became a real problem. Of course Bird was missing in action, leaving the rest of the guys stuck with doing the dirty work. He could usually be found "making out" somewhere with his just-discovered new girlfriend. The crime usually took place in his car or in the shadows somewhere else outside. Bird would return to the stage just in time for nothing left to be done, smiling, with his hair all messy, smelling like a whorehouse and staggering like a drunkard. Craze thought, "I guess this is what it's like having a kid; so, at this point, I'm thinking maybe I don't want any. So far, so good, with the Volcano, but I'm detecting smoke."

Lawder, the taskmaster, took these crimes particularly hard, and he always shot daggers from his eyes in the direction of the violator. So after several violations of "the rules," the Volcano decided, "I'm keeping track of these infractions from now on, and something's gonna be done about it."

Craze thought, "Bird's like kindling; he gonna get burned, and he's not even aware of it. His life is at stake. I don't think that this poor little Birdie has many days left on earth. But when the Volcano erupts, I'm not gonna help; I don't like getting burned... he's on his own."

Because of Bird's discipline problems, the band added fines. Lawder announced, "If you break the rules, you get fined; just that simple, and I'm the one who's gonna keep track."

Two reasons for the added fines: Number one, keep Bird in line, and number two and more importantly, KEEP HIM ALIVE.

"He has no shame in letting us do the dirty work, so let him pay for his sins," Craze thought. "It's a miracle that Lawder hasn't killed him yet."

Craze figured that by adding fines, Lawder had an outlet for his frustrations and a way of protesting Bird's behavior without getting physical. (In the end, Birdman held the distinction of being the most fined guy in the history of the band). Craze thought, "The weirdest thing is that every time Bird gets fined, he acts shocked and pissed. The look on his face says, 'How dare these guys have the gall to take my money. What did I do?'"

Bird became an important part of the band, but he never became part of the brotherhood.

𝄞

Located on the lower level of a strip mall, *The Castaways Club* became one of *The Public Service's* regular stops. Sometimes they opened up for acts like *Albert King, The Hour Glass, The Box Tops, Question Mark and the Mysterians, Blood, Sweat and Tears,* and *The Flock,* featuring *Jerry Goodman;* so the place rocked.

One night, *The Public Service* played a solo gig at *The Castaways*, so they occupied the stage for the entire evening, which included four sets with three breaks. Because the band played there so often, they felt comfortable with the surroundings. On this particular night, Bird might have gotten a little too comfortable because he pulled an unusual amount of "Bird shenanigans." He came back late after every break. He even committed the cardinal sin of horsing around on his guitar between songs.

Lawder got more and more aggravated with every infraction. Looking like a flashing-red stoplight and warning Craze of the impending disaster, Lawder's ears and face flashed on and off red throughout the night. Relieved that the gig had ended, and thinking the danger had passed, Craze let his guard down.

"Thank God that's over with," he thought. "I don't know how much more pressure I could have taken. 'Oh well, all's well that ends well.'"

Thinking that the whole episode was over, Craze, along with the rest of the band EXCEPT BIRD, busily packed their gear. Worrying again, Craze pondered, "Where is that guy? Hasn't he caused enough damage already?"

While Craze packed his drums, he heard mumbling coming from Lawder's direction: "Where is that little SOB? He hasn't packed a thing. Who does he think he is leaving me here doing all the hard work while he's out gallivanting around with some little chickie-poo? Well, I'll show him, I'll get Craze to fine that little bastard."

By now, Lawder's ears and face glowed lava red. His ranting got the attention of the rest of the guys. Nobody looked up, fearing eye contact with the Volcano; they just continued packing, pretending as if they did not hear his ranting. Lawder finished packing first and walked over to Peter's *Hammond* Organ. Sizing it up, he quietly muttered, "Hey, I need some help getting this thing up the steps."

The guys in the band feared responding, so they all continued packing, ignoring Lawder's request. Lawder quietly repeated, "Hey guys, will somebody PLEASE help me move this damn *Hammond* out of here?"

From past experiences, fear held the scared band members back from responding.

Finally, the Volcano blew, blacking out, and spewing an ear-splitting noise, "WELL, I GUESS NOBODY'S GONNA HELP, so I guess I'll just have to get this thing by myself."

The rest of the band looked over in astonishment. Lawder picked up the *Hammond* organ from under the keyboard, ALL BY HIMSELF, and leaned backwards straining from the weight. Lawder lugged the *Hammond* off the stage, across the dance floor, and proceeded to the long, steep stairs leading out of the lower level. Craze ran ahead and beat the Volcano to the stairs, while the other two guys followed a safe distance behind the eruption. Craze got to the top of the steps, looked down and considered, "They're too steep for one guy, and that organ is one bulky piece of equipment; it usually takes at least four people to move that thing. My odds say that he ain't gonna make it. If he falls backwards, those two down below (Eyes and Peter) are gonna get squashed!"

As Lawder miraculously reached the top of the stairs, the glowing Volcano screamed, "That little Bird-turd is gonna wish he was dead after I get done with him."

Craze ran into the parking lot, and quickly surveyed the terrain. "That must be Bird in that car with the fogged-up windows."

Craze banged on the passenger's door window screaming, "Bird, is that you? If it is, get out of here now."

The window rolled down and there sat Birdman with a stupid look on his face and a hickey on his neck. Shocked by the interruption, Bird peered out the window and in a perplexed tone asked, "What?" Craze shouted back, "Get out of here immediately. You're really screwed now. Lawder's gonna be here any second and if he spots you, you're dead."

Sobering up and realizing his dilemma, Bird asked, "What did I do?" Now panicking, and facing the girl in the driver's seat, Bird nervously asked, "Hey man, do me a favor; get me outta here like right now, okay?"

As Birdman escaped out of the parking lot, Craze shouted at the car, "By the way, you're fined five dollars."

Bird shouted back, "What did I do?"

Reaching the door at the top of the stairs with Eyes and Peter not far behind, the Volcano flowed across the parking lot and dumped its organ-load into the van. With Lawder now empty-handed, and fearing what might come next, the three remaining guys retreated back down the steps to the safety of the stage. They quickly finished packing, loaded the rest of the equipment, and locked themselves in the van. They looked out the windows for Lawder, but he had disappeared. Not knowing what to do next, the three guys drove out of the parking lot. Craze said, "I don't know, maybe he's walking home; maybe we'll see him on the way home? Well, it looks like Bird survived another day so that he can drive Lawder nuts again."

The next day, Craze got a call from Lawder. In a calm voice, he asked, "You did fine Bird, didn't you?"

Knowing the repercussions of the wrong answer, and relieved that he had officially fined Bird in the parking lot, Craze confidently stated, "Yes."

For years, no one ever mentioned the subject of that night… and nobody ever found out how Lawder or Bird for that matter got home that night.

CHAPTER 7

Bird proudly dragged in his new four-foot-tall dummy speaker cabinet. Out of breath, he said, "Man, that's real heavy. We built it out of two by fours and three-quarter-inch plywood. That ought to do the trick."

Bird had another nasty trick up his sleeve. (Never missing a chance "To pick up an extra buck," Bird, Peter, and Craze taught music lessons to younger kids.) "I'm gonna borrow one of my student's cheap guitars and use it to knock over the dummy. I'm not using my *Strat*, that's for sure."

Being a Pete Townsend fan, Bird continued, "Now I can do my own '*Who* destruction act' with this baby and never hurt the thing; it's built like a tank. Look at that covering; we got the stuff straight from *Fender*. It looks real, don't you guys think?"

Impressed, the rest of the guys shook their heads, "Yes!"

Craze booked a gig at Eyes's, Lawder's, and Craze's old junior high. Mr. Quist, the short, big-nosed "short-man syndrome" vice principal of the school met them at the door. "I hope you gentlemen don't plan on playing too loudly tonight, do you?"

Craze thought, "Up yours!" but replied, "Oh no, we wouldn't think of doing such a thing."

Entering the gym, Craze's mind flashed back to three years ago when he stood in line for gym class and Mister Quist informed his gym class that President Kennedy had been shot. Craze realized that Bird had placed his dummy-speaker box on a two-foot riser, on the exact spot where Coach had stood that day and accused Craze's gym class of being responsible for the assassination. After Mr. Quist had left, Coach shouted, "I knew that it would come to this! The youth of America is the downfall of this country and 'your kind' is responsible for what just happened!"

Craze never forgave that statement.

While the other band members set up on the riser, Bird carefully placed the dummy-amp on the end of the stage and out of the way of all the other instruments, saying, " This finale will be perfect! I can't wait for the BIG SURPRISE."

That evening, the guys had a ball playing for the younger crowd at their old junior high. Throughout the night, the gym floor filled with dancers and everybody had a good time. Mr. Quist only told the band three times, "Pipe down, pipe down you're way too loud."

Finally, as the evening ended, the band prepared for the "well-planned" grand finale. Birdman switched guitars and launched into his tirade...then Bird went off script and things immediately headed south. He smashed the borrowed guitar into pieces, throwing the scraps to the adoring crowd for souvenirs. Bird screamed, "They aren't ever going to forget this night if I have anything to say about it."

Skeptical about the whole thing in the first place, Lawder watched as Bird completely lost control. Now, guitar-less, Bird turned and shoved the dummy amp off the back of the stage. Pushing too hard, Bird disappeared off the back of the stage with the amp.

That's when things went very, very wrong. Somehow, a cord from another amp had gotten wrapped behind the dummy amp, and the entire bank of amps fell like dominos off the back of the stage. Sticking to their original plan and not wanting to ruin the moment, the band jumped off the stage, like nothing unexpected had just happened, ran out the gym door, leaving their adoring crowd behind cheering at the spectacle they had just witnessed. After digging his way out of the pile of amps, Bird followed staggering out the door behind the rest of the guys. The band left the pile of buzzing amps behind and vacated the premises as if in triumph.

Craze thought, "Now I know what they mean when they say, 'no matter what, the show must go on.' We couldn't let the audience know that the whole thing was a mistake!"

CHAPTER 7

Except for Lawder, the guys gathered outside in the parking lot, feeling sick about what had just happened. The Volcano vented around the parking lot spewing obscenities, kicking and swinging at everything in sight. As the realization of this blunder sunk in, each member of the band started calculating in their mind just how much this gaffe might have cost them. After the crowd dispersed, the band returned to the scene of the crime with the amps still buzzing on the floor.

Peter said, "Well, that's a good sign, at least some of them are still working."

Blessed by the gods, little damage occurred to their precious equipment. Later, when Bird's student inquired about his guitar, Bird replied, "I lost it." Slipping his victim a couple of bucks Bird stated, "That piece of junk wasn't really wasn't worth much anyway. Here, use this for a down payment and get yourself a good guitar."

𝄞

For years a rumor floated around the city about how the *Sunset Country Club* got started. The story suggested that Gussy Busch, *The King of Beers* and owner of *The St. Louis Cardinals*, attempted to join the prestigious *St. Louis Athletic Club*. Because his family came from "new money," the club rejected his application. So rumor had it that Gussy formed his own private club to "spit in the eye" of the old St. Louis money-tycoons.

The new assignment for *The Public Service*: "Play for the rich kids at *Sunset*."

The Public Service set up on the afternoon of the gig. At the time, the band used a ploy that got them free help, and at the same time allowed a couple of their fans to attend certain private events. If the free labor helped the band set up as "band boys," a term used by many bands describing this privilege, they could go to the gig with the band (The big-time bands used the much more civilized term "equipment managers" or "roadies."). But the band used "band boys," which seemed perfectly acceptable at the time. As far as the guys could tell, this act became a status symbol for those who were chosen. Often, several male fans approached the band saying, "Can I be your 'band boy' some time?"

When approached, Craze took down their number and said, "We'll see; I'll put you on the list. You think you can pick up this heavy stuff and not break anything?" All inquirers unanimously answered with a firm, "Well yeah, I'm real strong." And, "I promise I'll be real careful."

So when needed, Craze pulled out the list and made phone calls, granting this "badge of honor" to the lucky recipients. This time Craze chose Booby, a childhood friend from the neighborhood with a bad foot. Craze thought, "He's next on the list and he's real loyal; we couldn't find a better fan. His bad foot never stopped him from doing anything else, so I'm sure he'll do fine."

Craze also chose Michael Granda, a long-wavy-haired, ponytailed kid with a tall, thin, lanky stature. Craze thought, "Man this kid has crashed every party that we've ever played at anyway; I wonder how he gets into all these private gigs? He'll probably be there anyway, so I know that he'll gladly help."

The two chosen honorees joined the band that afternoon and helped set up. That evening, Craze met the rest of the guys and the two band boys at a local burger joint. Pulling into the parking lot, Craze noticed Peter and Michael Granda talking by Peter's van. Michael held a small drum in his hand. Joining the conversation, Craze overheard Michael Granda stating, "Hey man, look what I bought this afternoon. It's an Indian drum called a 'tabla'; isn't it cool?"

Craze interrupted, "Yeah man that's really cool. You mind if I borrow it for a couple of weeks?"

As Bird did, Craze borrowed stuff from their fans on occasion. Craze thought, "Yeah, but I take care of their possessions."

Michael Granda replied, "Sure man, take it."

CHAPTER 7

Craze threw the small drum in his car. (By the way, forty years later, Craze finally remembered to return the tabla to Michael.) When the band finished their burgers, the entourage headed for the gig.

Setting up early allowed the band to use their previously successful ploy of showing up at the last minute, storming the room and beginning to play before anybody knew what hit them. Upon arrival, the guys jumped out of their vehicles and stormed inside. Armed with their tuned guitars around their necks, the guys entered the venue and got their desired response. Craze sat down behind his drum set and prepared to count down the first song. But Eyes stopped the band in their tracks.

"Hey man, my new 'echo machine' is missing," he announced.

The expensive piece of equipment that Eyes had just purchased had disappeared, blowing the intro and leaving the audience even more confused. The band left the stage and approached the management. Eyes started the conversation by saying, "What happened to our echo machine? I thought you guys were watching our stuff? We've never lost anything before. The establishment always protects our equipment when we're not here."

The manager responded, "We don't know anything about what happened to your piece of equipment. Maybe those two guys took it. Who are they?" and pointed to Michael and Booby.

Now really hot, Eyes demanded, "Those guys are our 'band boys' and they've been with US the whole time. They didn't take it. We need to search the place. Maybe it's still here. Let's go search the employee lockers. It might be hidden there."

"Well sir, that's against the law and besides, our employees are honest and wouldn't do such a thing," the manager replied.

Stalemated by the manager, the band grudgingly faced the fact nothing could be done about the lost echo machine.

In the background, Craze noticed that Booby had paid close attention to the argument. Frustrated, the band returned to the stage and played the gig because it was the professional thing to do; and besides, now they needed the money to replace the stolen echo machine.

At some point, Craze noticed that Booby had disappeared. The guys in the band didn't give it much thought until the end of the gig. After the gig, Eyes gathered the band around and said, "You know, I think my parents have insurance for this kind of thing, so we might come out all right."

Feeling a little relieved about the disaster, Craze asked, "Anybody seen Booby? I could use some help?"

Booby finally reappeared smiling, and acting proud of himself. He climbed on stage and proudly announced, "I took care of those SOBs for you guys. I got a can of 10w30 out of my trunk and filled up the 18th hole with motor oil. The first guy that sinks that 18th hole is gonna get a real surprise…that'll show 'em. Then I did a few donuts on a couple of their greens with my car just to make sure they got the point."

Eyes responded, "We better get outta here."

Michael Granda, the other band boy…well that's a completely different story.

Chapter 8

Daredevils and *The King*

Years later, Craze moved to the university town of Columbia, Missouri, and played with a new band named *The Hard Corp*. A bluegrass-picking friend of the band recommended that they go see "a cool band." "I guarantee you'll love them," he said.

The friend, a man of few words, seldom spoke, so when he said something, everybody listened. Craze figured that this band with the cool name must be a bluegrass band. Craze really preferred rock to bluegrass, but he thought, "What the heck, we're going as a band; so I'll tag along."

The guys in Craze's new band entered the venue located on the university campus. Craze sat down and prepared for an evening of bluegrass music. The *Daredevil* guys entered the stage, took their positions and prepared to play. A tall, lanky guy stood front and center on stage and approached the mic. With his bass guitar slung behind him on his back, he spoke, "Welcome Columbia…my name is 'Supe' and we're the *Ozark Mountain Daredevils*."

Supe paused, swinging his bass guitar into playing position, then returned to the mic. He continued, "MOST BANDS PLAY ROCK. WE PLAY ROLL…"

After the introduction they busted into their song "If You Want to Get to Heaven, You've Got to Raise a Little Hell." Overwhelmed by the cool song, Craze settled in, anticipating a great evening of music.

Craze surveyed the guys on stage and their laid-back way of presenting their music. He thought, "This guy in front named Supe looks so familiar. Where do I know...wait a minute...that's Michael...Michael our 'OLD BAND BOY!'"

Craze flipped out, "It's MICHAEL GRANDA. I haven't seen him for years. I didn't even know he played bass guitar."

As the music continued, one great song after another, Craze's mind wandered back to *The Public Service* days: "He was at every gig; he was there so often that he became a like a fixture. He came up to me so often saying, 'Hey Craze, how you doin?' that I got used to saying, 'How you doin' kid?' and went about my business. I got so used to him being there all the time that I kind of took Michael for granted. So here I sit listening as his fan, and there he stands playing his new hit songs. It goes to show you, YOU NEVER KNOW. I'll NEVER take anybody for granted again."

After *The Daredevils'* show, Craze and his new band went backstage. Surrounded by their adoring fans, Michael and his band members enjoyed the moment. Craze joined the fans around Michael and slowly made his way to the front of the crowd. Finally face to face with Supe, Craze got his attention by announcing, "Michael, how you doin'?"

Supe, extremely busy giving his fans his total attention, took one look at Craze and replied, "How you doin' kid?" and returned his focus to his admirers.

Humbled and humored, Craze thought, "So who's the big shot now?"

Craze faded into the background, taking pleasure in the festivities. Later, the crowd thinned, and Supe spotted Craze sitting at a table with a smile on his face. He sat down next to Craze and they talked. Supe said, "Hey man, 'long-time-no-see.' How have you been? I heard *The Public Service* broke up. Have you heard from the guys? How are they doing?"

Craze responded, "Oh, everybody's fine, we keep in touch; but we're all going in different directions. I ended up here in Columbia going to school and playing with *The Hard Corp*."

Supe replied, "Wow, I didn't know you were playing with those guys. That's really cool. The guys in that band have followed your lead singer for years and love his music. I moved to Springfield after high school and got together with these guys. We're doing pretty good; things are getting real exciting."

Craze said, "Man, I bet they are. That's great. Now, I have another question. What's with this 'Supe' thing?"

Supe responded, "Yeah, well a bunch of people kept saying I looked like a bowl of soup on stage. It caught on, so I changed my name to 'Supe'."

Craze flashed back to the lanky kid who followed the band around and replied, "That's cool man."

𝄞

But before Craze even moved to Columbia, the popularity of *The Public Service* steadily increased and jobs became more plentiful. Armed with their new Nero Jackets made by Lawder's mom, the new-look band increased their schedule, including some weeknight gigs. The expanded schedule took a toll on the guys, who were still in high school. One bad experience caused by breaking a major rule of all musicians—"always take care of your instrument first"—almost cost Craze everything.

Finishing the weeknight gig, Craze returned home in the wee hours of the morning. He had one more task left before hitting the sack: unload the drums out of his car. But on this occasion, he rationalized, "Man I'm dead tired, I'll unpack my drums in the morning before school. Right now, I need to get some sleep, and I've only got a few hours before school starts. I'm just too tired."

He parked in the back yard so that nobody could see his car from the street. The number two most important rule: "Do not let weeknight gigs get in the way of school."

His parents and the other guys' parents allowed the weeknight gigs as long as they did not get in the way of school.

The next morning, Craze woke up late in a panic. He ran outside and got in his car. Waking up a little bit and wiping the sleep out of his eyes, he saw the drums in the back seat and realized his dilemma. He made a split-second decision. "I'm already late; I'll have to leave the drums in the car."

As he pulled out of the driveway, he rationalized, "I mean what could possibly happen? What are the chances of a bad guy seeing the drums in the car anyway?"

Craze took a huge risk and drove to school. He found a "safe place" to park on a side street. He thought, "Phyllis Diller, the comedian, lives on this street, for crying out loud. It's a great neighborhood. How much safer could a parking place be?"

Convincing himself this was almost as secure as the basement, he locked the car, left his drum-filled vehicle on the street and ran to the closest door of the high school. After school, casually walking down the tree-lined street with mansions, Craze enjoyed the crisp fall day. When he got to the spot, his heart froze. The parking space sat empty before him, now occupied only by an old oil smudge left long ago. Stunned, he scratched his head and quickly assessed his bleak state of affairs.

"Well I was in a hurry, maybe I parked it in another place; I WAS pretty tired. Maybe I parked somewhere else. That's it! I just forgot where I parked."

For the next hour, Craze walked all around the high school checking every spot he had ever parked and some that he had never used. He checked everywhere, but his drum-filled Chevy convertible had disappeared. Now sick to his stomach, a harsh reality set in.

"Everything I own just vanished off the face of the planet. My entire existence is gone."

Not really knowing what to do next, he walked home contemplating his predicament. Entering the door of his house, he walked to the phone and called the police, figuring that his hard-earned belongings were somewhere in East St Louis. Kicking himself for being so stupid, he sat there pondering a life without all of his worldly belongings. "If I had had a hole, I'd crawl in it."

Hopeless, Craze sat in his room thinking, "Man, I'm gonna have to work and save a lot to dig myself out of this one. What a dim-witted move. I knew better and now look at the fix I'm in."

A few hours later, his mom hollered upstairs, "Craze, the police are on the phone, hurry up."

Flying down the stairs, Craze thought, "Well I guess they've got more questions."

He picked up the phone and said, "Hello, this is Craze speaking?"

The voice on the other end of the phone replied, "Hello, Mr. Craze, this is the police department. I'm calling to tell you that we found your car. It was located three blocks from where you said it was stolen. If you can get over there, there's an officer waiting at the scene."

With a thousand questions on his mind, Craze said, "Thank you, I'll be right over," and hung up.

His dad gave him a ride to "the scene of the crime" while Craze leaned forward in his seat trying to make the car go faster. Before the car came to a complete stop, Craze jumped out of the car and ran to his Chevy, saw the drums in the back seat and checked the car for dents or scratches.

"Thank you Lord, the drums are still there and I don't see any damage. They didn't even hurt the ignition key," Craze thought.

The policeman said, "You're a lucky young man. Most of the

time, these things don't turn out so good. These convertibles are easy to break into. I'm guessing the car ran out of gas. Is that a possibility?"

Craze smiled to himself and stated, "Yes. That is entirely possible."

The cop left the scene and Craze's dad took him to the filling station to buy some gas.

Driving home, Craze thought about his near disaster. He usually gave his sister's friends a ride home after school and charged them a quarter apiece. Those four or five quarters usually bought enough gas for Craze to bomb around for a while and still have enough gas left to get to school the next morning. Sometimes he ran out of gas before he got to the filling station. In that case, he sat in his car while the girls ran to get more gas with their quarters. Craze thought, "It's a pretty good system, and who would have ever thought that this routine would save my skin."

𝄞

In the 1950s, Albert King started out as a Caterpillar Operator. He kept that day job until he could make a living playing his beloved blues full-time. On stage, his left-handed *"Flying V" Gibson guitar*, his large frame and his huge smile created an impressive image on stage. Front and center in his black tux, Albert's presence literally overwhelmed any venue. His deep, booming, voice and room-filling smile mesmerized his audience into focusing on every word he spoke, while his vocals pierced their souls. As commander of his own personal blues vessel, Albert's dominating gestures guided his sharp-looking, black tuxedo-dressed band through every move.

Albert drew his band to a whisper and told great stories about lost loves, heartbreaks and missing his "Main Squeeze," the woman in his life. He would claim, "It's been three long weeks today since I've seen my 'Main Squeeze' and that's what's known as the blues."

After his story, Albert's band exploded full-volume for the climax of each song. Saving the best for last, and accenting the tale he had just told, Albert wailed distinctive leads on his companion, his *Flying V Gibson*. His performances lured the audience in, then blew them away with his killer guitar leads. Albert King's distinctive guitar style strongly influenced popular artists like Stevie Ray Vaughn, Johnny Winter and other major artists. In Craze's eyes, "Albert King was the best blues artist of his generation."

𝄞

The Mississippi River created almost unbearable humidity that evening in the city. *The Public Service* escaped into the cool basement of *The Castaways Club*, excited about the evening ahead. Ignoring the heat outside, the band prepared for that night's booking: backing up the great *Albert King*. Peter and his brother Paul knew Albert's music well because in their younger days, their father insisted that the two boys listen to Albert's radio shows. Eyes and Craze witnessed Albert's magic in "black establishments" like *The Moonlight Lounge* and *The Grand Masonic Lodge*. Sometimes these shows included other famous blues artists like Mississippi Fred McDowell, Jimmy Reed, and John Lee Hooker. But on this night, *The Public Service* had the honor of sharing the stage with Albert.

As with B.B. King and other blues artists of the time, the introduction of white audiences created new opportunities for Albert. His music and personality made quite an impression on the national level. Soon after this gig, Albert planned his first national tour showcasing his new album *Live Wire Blues Power*. After finishing their set, *The Public Service* joined Albert backstage while his band set up.

As Craze entered the room, he thought, "Wow, this is unexpected, I didn't think we'd get the honor of spending personal time with Albert. This is gonna be cool."

The Great Albert King sat before them looking sharp as usual in his black tux. Albert's large frame occupied the couch, the WHOLE couch. Craze thought, "He's as large in real life as he is on stage. Maybe it's the small room. Whatever, I don't think I'll ever forget this moment." Little did he know how true that statement would become!

His huge smile and impressive stature greeted the band as they entered the room. Albert looked at them, sizing them up. He waited for the band to enter the room before he slowly spoke: "Come on in boys and take a seat. Now boys, I was listening to your music and you just done three blues numbers, all in the same key. Now don't do that. This is the blues and you can't ever do that to your audience. You got to mix it up, never three tunes in the same key, never, never. Now promise me, please don't do that again."

The King had spoken and the band shook their heads in agreement. It never happened again.

After his lecture, he looked right at Craze. In his booming voice, Albert said, "Boy, come over here, and sit by me."

Craze looked behind him thinking that Albert might be talking to someone behind him. "No boy, I mean you," Albert said.

Craze shyly obeyed, taking a seat along side *The King*. Craze thought, "Why does he want to talk to me? Did I do something wrong? That has to be it. These other guys in the band are the great musicians, so that must be it. I screwed something up."

Sitting down, Craze focused his attention on Albert. Albert King said, "Son, I got an idea and I wanted to see what you thought about it. I like the way you play and you're just the type of drummer I'm looking for. So why don't you JOIN MY BAND. I'll pay you a hundred dollars a week and show you the world."

"What?" Craze thought. "Did I hear him wrong? Did the greatest blues player I've ever heard just say what I thought he said?"

Craze's system momentarily went into shock. Did *Albert King* just ask him to play in his band? As the reality of these words sunk in Craze thought, "This is way beyond anything that I could have ever imagined. Albert King himself just paid me the greatest compliment of my entire life."

Craze fell back in his chair and thought about what had just happened. He meekly responded, "Thanks Albert, but I'm only seventeen and I'm still in high school."

"What else was I supposed to say?" Craze thought to himself.

Albert responded with his huge smile and a slight laugh, "Oh, I can show you things that you would never see in high school. The world is a big place and high school can't teach you as much as I can. I'll show you places, and teach you things that you never dreamed of."

Craze slowly responded, "Thanks Albert, you just paid me a great compliment, but I can't do it. You know, my parents and all…"

"Well okay then, I understand," Albert answered. "But if you ever change your mind, look me up. Well it's time to go to work."

Albert got up and headed for the stage with *The Flying V* around his neck, leaving Craze behind fused to his seat. Albert entered the stage with his fans cheering him on while Craze sat, too dumbfounded to move.

Six months later and fresh off his tour, Albert appeared again at the same club. This time he sported a blond, long-haired new drummer; a hot young percussionist from L.A. Craze stood in the audience with the rest of the crowd, realizing that he had a different perspective on that concert. Nobody else knew what he knew. Craze thought while listening to his hero, "That could have been me up there."

Craze mentioned to Eyes: "Man, it's been a long time since we've played in front of our hometown crowd. Wouldn't it be cool to go back to where the whole thing started and do a gig at the Y again?"

Eyes replied, "That would be cool. We might have to take a cut in pay, but personally, I think it would be worth it. I bet the rest of the guys would agree. Why don't you make that happen, and I'll take care of the rest of the guys."

So Craze booked the *Webster YMCA* for the band's triumphant return home. As the gig-date got closer, the guys got more excited and decided to pull out all the stops.

Eyes said, "Let's do the old trick of you guys pulling up on your bikes and we'll follow in the van. Buck and Ralph (their new permanent equipment managers) can have the stuff ready, and we'll storm in, and play before anybody knows what hit them."

Lawder replied, "Man getting those guys for equipment managers is one of the best moves we ever made. You know, Buck and Ralph put the old days to rest of being worn out sweaty messes before we even started playing. And after the gig's over, they tear it all down and we get to go home."

Peter said looking at Bird with questioning eyes: "Yeah, and Bird, bring your dummy amp, and we'll do the destruction act again, but this time, no mistakes, okay?"

Bird stated with a slight smile, "Okay man, I promise. Hey, maybe I'll 'borrow' another guitar."

The afternoon before the gig, the guys entered the Y for set up. When they entered the room, several kids were busy working on the stage. They carefully lined the walls of the stage with aluminum foil creating a large mirror behind the band. Impressed with these kids' work, the band got even more excited about the coming evening.

That evening, before the gig, the band gathered at Craze's house, while Buck and Ralph went ahead, and got things ready at the Y. Eyes announced, "It's time."

Eyes and Craze led the way on their bikes while the rest of the guys followed in Peter's van. Surprising the fans, the band blasted into the parking lot and stormed into the front door. They pushed through the crowd and got on stage. With the instruments tuned and ready, they fired up their song before the audience knew what hit them. Throughout the evening, the crowd responded with affection to their hometown celebrities.

Before the finale, Eyes looked back at Bird and said, "You ready? Don't blow it this time or it'll cost you more than five bucks." Bird licked his chops and replied, "Let's do it. I already got the borrowed guitar ready."

As planned, Bird attacked the dummy-amp with ferocity. On cue, he knocked over the amp. As it fell to the floor, it tore a huge hole in the foil-lined wall. Seeing an opportunity, Bird attacked the rest of the foil with the head of his borrowed guitar, ripping huge chunks off the wall.

Eyes followed suit by wadding up the foil and throwing the "foil-wads" into the crowd. The fans fought for the hunks of foil like they were real chunks of silver. After ripping all the foil off the wall, Bird smashed the borrowed guitar to pieces and threw the remains into the crowd. Finishing the final song, the guys jumped off stage and departed the same way they had entered, pushing through their fans and leaving the building. They waited outside and greeted the fans as they left the Y.

Many years later, when their parents decided to sell "the old barn," Craze and his brother cleaned out their old rooms in their parents' attic. As his brother went through his chest of drawers, he pulled out a wad of foil. Getting Craze's attention and pointing to the chunk, his brother said, "Hey look what I found!"

His brother finished saying, "Man, that was a night to remember..."

𝄞

As Craze walked down the "gang plank" to the shiny, stainless steel riverboat, memories of his childhood filled his head. He looked back to shore and saw the almost completed *Gateway Arch* directly behind him. Craze thought, "Tonight we play on *The Admiral*, a dream come true. As a kid, I had so much fun on this boat. Taking a trip on *The Admiral* was as much fun as going to *The Lake of the Ozarks* or *Grant's Farm*; and now we get to play in "the Ballroom," one of the coolest rooms I've ever seen."

The Admiral stood out on the riverfront because of its unusual art deco design and shiny stainless steel exterior. The boat was moored right below *The Arch*, and Craze thought about the two landmarks: "With their shiny stainless steel exteriors, they kind of match; they really do make the riverfront shine in more than one way."

Once inside the riverboat, The Blue Salon Ballroom always impressed Craze. He thought back to the first time that he walked into the magnificent room. "As a kid, I thought this place was one of the most beautiful places that I've ever been. I remember asking my mom 'what is this place?' and she answered, 'Well Craze, it's called an 'art deco ballroom.'"

Not knowing what "art deco" meant, or for that matter what "ballroom" meant, he accepted the answer and went about his business; but the words stuck in his mind. He later found out what each word meant, and since that moment, "art deco" became his favorite art form.

After setting up, the guys began their performance. Relying more and more on reflecting their own personal identity, their music had taken a turn. They had slowly replaced the old British invasion influences with their own self-discovered blues songs. During their first set, they proudly displayed their new blues-influenced personality. After the first song, Craze noticed the captain rushing across the dance floor, heading in their direction. Eyes leaned down from the stage, and the captain whispered in his ear. With a flustered look in his face, Eyes gathered the band together. Talking softly so that the audience did not hear, Eyes said, "Man, you're not gonna believe what that guy just told me. He said, 'quit playing that jig-a-boo music, we don't want to make the jungle bunnies restless.'"

With their bubble burst and all the fun and excitement gone, the band finished the gig playing their old British music.

After doing some checking around, Craze found out that *The Admiral* had been one of the last segregated venues in the area and had recently been forced to integrate.

"I just don't get it," Craze thought. "What's wrong with these people?"

Figure 10. The *Admiral*, Arch, and Old Courthouse. *Courtesy of Christine Sydow.*

Figure 11. "Blue Salon" ballroom on the *Admiral*.
Courtesy of Christine Sydow.

Over the years, the topic of segregation often popped into Craze's mind. "Some of my closest friends are black, and I thought everything was just fine. But I never thought about it from their perspective; I never thought about what they had to go through. We actually were 'so close, but so far away' by living in different worlds so to speak. Thinking back, I'm embarrassed that I saw the world through rose-colored glasses and took things so lightly. I guess I never took the time to see the world from their perspective."

Thinking about that night on *The Admiral*, Craze concluded, "And just think, right on top of the hill behind *The Arch* is where the Dred Scott Decision took place at The Old Court House. Maybe things haven't really changed that much after all."

Craze came up with an idea: He sat down with the band and made his proposal: "I've got an idea about how we can expand our horizons and see how good we really are at the same time. I just got an invitation to compete in a 'Battle of the Bands' on the other side of the river in north East Saint Louis, at a place called *The Roundhouse*.

"I know that we've made it a rule to never play in 'battles' like this, and we only play gigs if the money is right. But think about this. The gig is far enough away that our fans won't show up; and if we win, we'll take home a pile of cash. We'll be the only band without fans. The other six bands will have fans; so how good do you guys really think we are? Can we go into enemy territory and steal the show? I think it's the perfect test. Let's take this gig and blow their doors off. What do you guys think?"

After a moment of silence, Eyes, with a glimmer of humor in his eye, spoke up, "What the hell, let's do it; and if we lose, we'll blame Craze and go home broke."

The rest of the guys agreed and decided to roll the dice.

The night of the gig, *The Public Service* pulled up to *The Roundhouse* and began unloading their equipment. As Craze unloaded his drums, he noticed Peter and Eyes talking. With Peter looking guilty and Eyes looking pissed, they approached the rest of the guys. Eyes said, "Tell 'em!"

With an embarrassed giggle, and making excuses, Peter meekly responded, "Well, I don't know how I could have done such a thing; I think that I might have been having an insulin reaction… but I ate a candy bar, and I feel much better now."

Eyes interrupted, "Just cut to the chase and tell 'em."

Still giggling, Peter finally fessed up, "Well guys, I forgot to pack the cord that attaches the *Hammond* to the *Leslie* speaker, which means we can't use the *Hammond*. I guess we'll just have to do without."

Lawder responded, "Well, go get it! We ain't playing without the *Hammond*, just go get the thing."

Peter replied, "But that's a three-hour-round trip; I might not make it back in time."

Lawder responded, "In that case, we'll just play without you; you're burning time, get moving!"

Peter said, "Well, okay then; I'll hurry."

Throughout the evening, Eyes and Craze made excuses about why they could not go on next. Three hours later, Peter pulled in just as the last band finished their set.

Finally, *The Public Service* took the stage and presented their act to the unfamiliar crowd. Eyes did his part pulling out all the stops, using his magnetism and charm to lure the audience to their side. The rest of the band played with authority, while Bird stole the girls' hearts. After the battle, the audience voted, and *The Public Service* walked away with the "Winner Take All" Prize.

During the evening, the band listened to their competition. A band called *The Purple Pig* had the biggest fan base, but a band called *The Black Zone* concerned them the most. Craze thought, "These guys are wild. I know we're better musicians, but they DO have a great show. I guess we'll just have to turn Eyes loose and let him charm the pants off of this audience."

That evening, a friendship blossomed between *The Public Service* and *The Black Zone*.

About a month later, their newfound friends invited *The Public Service* to join them in playing at a joint located in a seedy neighborhood called *The Club Illusion* in south East Saint Louis. On a bitterly cold night, both bands unpacked and gathered back-stage before the performance. Noticing the long bench with several round mirrors surrounded with light bulbs, Craze asked *The Black Zone* guys, "What's with the mirrors?"

One of the guys spoke up, "Oh yeah, this is an old strip club; the strippers got ready for their shows back here."

Some band members sat in chairs in front of the mirrors while others stood or milled about, as the usual "before-gig jitters" took hold. Craze thought while he hung out back stage, "There's really no place on earth like being backstage before a gig. With all the constant motion of shifting bodies and positive minds, the creative juices usually take over. You can feel brains waking up as wild-wit and humor rules the room. The air is filled with a kinetic energy just waiting to be released; but it's an inventive energy, kind of like 'plug me in, I'm ready.'"

On this particular night, on the spur of the moment, somebody mentioned that they needed a stage name. Craze remembered, "That's all it took to light the fuse." Names flew from every part of the room.

Somebody suggested, "How about Ben Dover or Chris Smith." Another suggestion: "I like I.P. Freely."

Other names were tossed about, like "Rock Bottom," "Rex Havoc," "A. Sphincter" and "Lou Stool." The riot continued until somebody said, "It's time to go on."

The mood immediately changed from tears of laughter to happy seriousness. With tears in his eyes, Craze left the room announcing his new stage name: "Buck Naked."

As the bands took their turns playing their sets, Craze thought, "Man, I love playing the East Side. On the other side of the river, in the city, for some reason, the crowds seem more judgmental, or somebody they respect has to tell them that bands are good before they are won over. These people on the East Side are here for one reason…HAVE FUN. And boy did everybody have fun tonight!"

And then the bands packed for their journey home.

The evening would have been perfect except for one small thing: Craze lost his car keys. The band ended up standing outside in the frigid conditions for hours, waiting for his mother to bring a spare set of keys from home. The band huddled in a "lean-to" built on the side of the building, all but Lawder, who chugged around the parking lot spewing steam like an old locomotive. Eyes shouted, "Lawder you're mental, get back in here. You're gonna freeze to death."

The happy Volcano replied, "Oh no, I kind of like the cold," as he continued chugging around the imaginary tracks in the parking lot until Craze's mom finally appeared.

The band returned home safely that night. The next day, Craze picked up his pants from the night before, and as he picked them up, he felt a bulge in the "watch pocket" above the pocket that he thought he had put his keys in. Reaching in with one finger, he pulled out the lost keys.

Armed with their new popularity on the East Side, things were about to get much better for *The Public Service*...except for Craze.

Figure 12. *Jefferson Airplane* poster.

Chapter 9

No Bummer Summer?

Craze stuck the drumsticks in the back pocket of his jeans and got on his motorcycle. "Man, this is so cool; the whole thing feels like a dream, and it's happening to US. It's the biggest night of our lives."

Craze thought as he left the record store armed with new drumsticks, "Okay man, now I'm ready. In a couple of hours we'll be on stage in front of hundreds of people."

Craze headed for home to get ready for the big night. About a half mile from the record store, Craze saw a cop parked on the side of the road in front of his high school; and, for an instant, he thought, "Do I have my helmet on? I got warned about not wearing a helmet a couple of weeks ago."

He looked back to the road just in time to see the car in the oncoming lane turn left in front of him.

In slow motion, Craze saw the front wheel of his bike smash into the back tire of the car. At the same time, he launched into the air and over the top of the car. Now air-born so many thoughts went through his head in such a short time. His mind raced, "So this is what it feels like to die. It didn't even hurt. I hear my bike grinding into that back wheel of the car."

Then, he heard the motorcycle engine stall. "So that means my bike just died. I guess I'm next. I think I saw an old man driving that car. I'm so calm and rational about this whole thing. What about tonight?"

Craze flew over the top of the car and landed on his head, rolled over on his back, then skidded down the pavement on his butt.

When Craze came to, dazed and confused, he removed his helmet and saw the crack caused by the impact. As the cop approached, Craze thought, "Well I'm not gonna lie here in the street. I'll just get up and walk over to the cop."

As he tried to get on his feet, the pain hit every part of his body, and he dropped in a heap like a newborn fawn attempting to walk for the first time. Then he thought as he fumbled for the sticks still in his back pocket, with his right hand, "I think I'm still alive...but I can't use my right hand."

As he painfully and unsuccessfully tried to move, he thought, "Man, what a fall; besides my wrist, every bone in my body hurts...but somehow, I'm still here."

Suddenly, flashes of the band's most recent rise in popularity blasted through his mind.

𝄞

"Man, what a perfect day," Craze thought. "I bet we'll have a huge crowd."

With the bitter cold of winter gone and clear blue skies and mild temperatures prevailing, the people of the city welcomed the cool spring days. *The Public Service* booked an outdoor concert at the crown jewel of the city, *Forest Park*.

That day, the band opened up for San Francisco's *Quicksilver Messenger Service*. *The Public Service* entertained one of their largest crowds to date, and the crowd had a positive response to their blues-oriented music.

As the guys packed their equipment in the vans, a wiry little guy pulled up on his *Honda 50* motorcycle. He removed his helmet, exposing his dark, wild hair. Craze thought, "This guy looks like a speed freak or maybe a cheap version of Bob Dylan."

The Dylan clone confidently approached the band and with self-assurance in his voice, announced, "Hey man, how you doing? I represent a company called *Velvet Plastic Productions*. Our production company has booked a series of concerts and my boss is interested in hiring *The Public Service* as the opening band for all the concerts."

The skinny guy handed a business card to Eyes and said, "Please call Jorge my boss, as soon as possible."

Being skeptical, Craze gave *Mr. Velvet Plastic* the band's standard answer: "Sure, thanks, we'll give you a call."

Craze took his card, and the guy got back on his bike and drove away. As the guy drove off, Eyes and Craze really did not give the encounter much thought. Standing next to Eyes, Craze said, "This little guy just doesn't fit my image of a big-time booking agent...and driving that puny *Honda 50* doesn't help the image much."

They looked at each other and shrugged. On more than one occasion, various characters had approached the band with "get rich quick schemes." These "schemes" always seemed to cost the band money; the profits always ended up in somebody else's pocket, not the band's. After thinking about this latest proposition, Craze said, "What do you think?"

Eyes replied, "Well Craze, I guess it wouldn't hurt to give this Jorge guy a call. I'm as sick as you are with all these 'fly-by-night big shots' trying to pick our pockets; but we can always say no . . . but YOU NEVER KNOW."

That next week, Craze called the *Velvet Plastic* number. A girl answered saying,

"*Velvet Plastic Productions*, this is Cosmos, can I help you?" Craze thought, "Well, she at least sounds legit."

"Hi, my name is Craze and I represent *The Public Service*. A guy gave me your card and said that I should call this number."

Cosmos replied, "Oh yes, we've been expecting your call. Would you like to make an appointment and meet with Jorge?"

Craze thought, "At least they sound real."

Eyes and Craze jumped on their motorcycles and drove to the address located across the street from the *Washington University* campus. Eyes said, "Well at least they have a decent location."

They opened the door and entered the office. Shocked by what they saw, they paused and took in the decor. Craze thought, "This doesn't look like any office I've ever seen before. It's way too cool to be called an office. It's more like an 'Indian Palace Office' or something." At that moment, they both realized that, "THIS JUST MIGHT BE THE REAL DEAL!"

A beautiful girl sat behind a desk made of clear plastic, which exposed all of the contents inside the desk drawers . . .and the beautiful girl herself. She said, "Greetings, I'm Cosmos. Please have a seat while I go get Jorge."

Craze thought, "So this Cosmos chick is who I talked to on the phone. She seems nice, and good-looking to boot. Man, this is the coolest office I've ever seen. But the only chair in this joint is Cosmos's cool, clear-plastic desk chair. I guess everybody else sits on these large hippie decorated cushions…I'm hip."

Craze and Eyes sat on the pillows while Cosmos left the room. Indian rugs covered the floor and walls, making the room bright and welcoming. The guys sat straining their necks, taking in all the cool stuff in the room. Besides the pillows and rugs, beads and trinkets hug from the ceiling glistening in the sunlight from the storefront window. Craze looked at Eyes and said softly, "Well, maybe *Mr. Velvet Plastic* wasn't blowing smoke after all." Eyes shook his head in agreement.

Smelling of patchouli oil, Jorge entered the room sporting long, curly black hair, bell-bottom jeans, a flowered shirt, and a brown leather vest. Short in stature, the dark-skinned Latino, Jorge, greeted the guys with a huge smile from under his large, black mustache.

"Welcome to *Velvet Plastic Productions,* I'm Jorge and I'm glad to meet you."

Eyes returned the greeting, "Hey man, I'm Eyes the singer and this is Craze, the drummer."

Jorge joined the two on the cushions with a folder tucked under his arm. Craze thought, "This feels like some Guru is getting ready to address his flock.

Jorge began, "I understand that my assistant contacted you in the park and passed on my message. I've heard *The Public Service* personally, and I enjoyed your music. I've checked around town, and you guys have an outstanding reputation. You also have quite a following, and that sparks my interest, and why you're here. I can use your popularity to attract more patrons.

"We've contracted several national acts, for example *The Grateful Dead, Jefferson Airplane, Canned Heat, and Steppenwolf.* I'm calling the concert series *No Bummer Summer.* We have other "big-name" contracts pending. But that's another story for another day. So with all that said, I'd like to sign you to a series of concerts opening up for these major acts."

Eyes and Craze sat momentarily speechless. Then Eyes spoke up. "Well, how much?"

After coming to an agreement on pay, Jorge opened up his folder and spoke, "Well gentlemen, is one of you over the age of 18? These are the contracts and you have to be at least 18 to make these binding."

Panic set in as Eyes and Craze looked at each other. Craze thought, "You're kidding me; we're too young to sign this? You're telling me we're gonna blow this because we're too young? Our dream is right in front of us and we can't even make it happen. Man, this is NOT cool."

Eyes leaned forward and took over the conversation. In his best businesslike voice he said, "Well, neither of us is 18, but let me ask you this. Can we get another party to sign for us, like a parent or something?" Jorge thought for a second and replied,

"Yeah, sure, I'd accept a parent's signature. How soon can you get a parent in here to sign?"

Eyes calmly replied, "Give us a couple of hours and we'll have somebody here to sign the contracts. Will that work for you?"

"I'll agree to that," Jorge said. "Now guys, I have to get back to work. I'll see you back here in a couple of hours."

Eyes and Craze walked out of the office. As soon as the door closed behind them, both guys ran to their bikes. Eyes said, "Let's blow this pop-stand; I got a plan. We need to get over to my house and pick up my mom. She'll sign; she just doesn't know it yet. Now keep up with me we're gonna break some laws."

Pulling in front of Eyes's house, both guys jumped off their bikes and ran through the front door. As they entered the kitchen, breathless, Eyes yelled, grabbing his mom's arm, "Mom you gotta come with us right now. Get in my car."

His mom Mary, with her apron still on, frantically said, "Eyes, Eyes, wait a minute, honey. What are you doing?"

"Don't worry about it. We'll explain everything on the way. Just get in the car. By the way, you got a pen on you?"

The hard work and discipline of *The Public Service* paid off as Mary, not really sure about what had just happened, signed the contracts. Eureka!

𝄞

At the scene of the accident and still confused, Craze refused an ambulance. His Grandpa Zak picked him up from the accident site and took him to the ER. After Craze returned home from the hospital with a fractured wrist, bummed up leg and raw backside, Eyes's girlfriend and her best friend picked up Craze and took him to the *Steppenwolf* concert.

He asked, "How did you know that I had a wreck?"

Eyes's girlfriend said, "Somebody saw the accident and called

Eyes. He sent us to check on you and bring you back if possible."

Craze replied, "Oh, I get it; well let's get going. By the way, who's playing the drums?"

Eyes's girlfriend responded, "Billy...Eyes will explain the whole thing later; but for now we've got to go or we'll miss the whole thing."

They arrived just in time to see the last set. Still in shock and taking pain pills, Craze vaguely remembered the girls wheeling him around in his wheelchair, dodging fans. Word had gotten back to the band about Craze's accident. At the last minute, they got a friend of the band named Billy to sub for Craze that night. When Craze found out about Billy taking his place, he wondered, "I heard that Billy played a keyboard, but I didn't know he played the drums. As a matter of fact, I'm not sure that he ever played in a band, let alone a crowd of this size."

Thinking about Billy's dilemma, Craze thought, "Man Billy's getting 'christened by fire' tonight. If anybody knows the music, he sure does because he's been around so much. God be with him."

The next day, the guys went over to Craze's house and they each took turns filling Craze in on the concert. Peter started, "Billy did real good man. The poor guy was scared to death, but he's a real good drummer and he knew all the stuff, so that helped a lot."

Craze replied, "I was worried about Billy. I'm relieved to hear that he did a good job."

Changing the subject, Peter continued, "Don't get me wrong, we had fun. But *Steppenwolf's* guitar player spilled a Coke on my *Hammond* and ruined the finish; he acted like it was no big deal. That really made me mad."

From past experience with Peter, Craze knew Peter was really pissed because he took good care of his equipment. Craze further thought: "When Peter says 'I'm really mad,' that's as mad as he gets. So he's not happy at all about what happened to the *Ham-*

mond. He really takes care of his stuff and I don't blame him."

Eyes spoke up next. "So, we get there and *Steppenwolf* is already set up, which I found unusual. There they were standing on the stage, looking all proud at their new equipment. Then one of the guys in the band announces that they want us to use their amps. He said that they had just sighed a new contract with an amp manufacturer and that this company frowns on any amp other than theirs being on stage. So they asked us to use their stuff. Well, I'm thinking, cool, less work on us.

"So we're doing a sound check and I look over at Lawder. He's turning knobs and turning red at the same time. I figure something's up. Well, I wasn't going to say anything; I'm not nuts. The next thing I know, Lawder's dragging the amp off stage and comes back with his own amp. Now I see he's happy and I think everything's cool."

At this point, Lawder took over and said, "I couldn't get my sound. I tried, but it just wasn't gonna work. So I think, 'no problem,' I'll just use my amp; problem solved. Well the bass player dude comes running on stage screaming, 'You can't do that, you can't do that, we have an agreement and you can't do that.' Well, I look at him and say 'Agreement my ass, this thing is a piece of crap and I ain't using it. If you want to use that piece of junk, go ahead, but I'm not; I don't care what damned kind of contract you guys signed…you got screwed. So get out of my face.'"

Now laughing, Lawder continued, "Well, I guess I scared the crap out of the poor guy. I never saw anybody tuck his tail between his legs and get off the stage so fast. Really, I didn't mean to scare him THAT bad, but he had it coming, don't you think?"

Craze shook his head in agreement, knowing better than to disagree. Eyes said, "Craze, I'm assuming we'll need to get Billy for *The Grateful Dead* concert in two weeks. What do you think?"

Determined, Craze replied, "No way man. I've missed enough. I'm playing that gig no matter what it takes."

Craze insisted that he play the show even though he had a cast on his wrist. With his wrist and knees still messed up, Craze went to his dad's workshop, took a hammer and smashed the cast on his wrist so that he had a little movement. Then he went to work practicing the drums with the deck stacked against him.

As he entered the backstage area, Craze saw the two *Dead* drummers warming up, doing paradiddles, flamadiddles, and double and single rolls in perfect synchronization. Craze thought, "I'm in big trouble."

Backstage, guys in *The Grateful Dead* treated the guys in *The Public Service* graciously, and they appreciated their respectful treatment. Craze liked Pig Pen the best. "The guy looks tough as nails," he thought. "But Pig Pen's like their host; he's making sure that we feel welcome and comfortable...what a nice guy."

The Public Service left the backstage area and entered the stage to set up and do a sound check. The first thing they noticed: Jerry Garcia sitting in a chair, stage left, warming up on his guitar. He stopped playing, put his guitar down, and introduced himself. "Hey guys, I'm Jerry."

The guys returned the introduction and Jerry spoke up again, "I'd like to talk to you guys and ask a favor. *The Dead* is known for our marathon concerts. So, when we get into the groove, we don't like stopping. If don't mind, would you do one set and we'll take over from there?"

The set-up for the two-day concerts required that the opening band play the first set, then the main act play the second set. The opening band then returned for the third set, and the main act returned for the finale. But *The Grateful Dead* and Jerry Garcia did not like the plan. Garcia asked, "So what do you guys think?"

The Public Service had no problem with his proposal, so Eyes responded, "What the hell, it pays the same; sounds good to me...it's a win/win, as far as we're concerned."

A few hours later, *The Public Service* took their positions on the dark stage. As Craze limped to his drum set, he thought, "Man, it's dark out here. I can barely find my way around."

In the darkness, Eyes signaled Craze and with the stick shoved in his crushed cast, Craze thought, "Well here we go."

Craze started the first song, clicking his sticks, one, two, three, four...simultaneously, the band hit the first note and the lights

Figure 13. *Grateful Dead* and *Public Service* flyer.

came up. Surprised and blinded by the brightness of the lights, and terrified, but ecstatic at the same time, Craze thought, "What a weird feeling; I can only see the first two rows, but I can sense the rest of this huge crowd, very cool."

As the band finished their first song and the applause began. Craze thought, "Man, this many people can make a lot of noise."

As tensions eased, the band fed off the energy of the crowd and went into attack mode. They finished the set without a hitch…except for Craze's arm and leg. He thought, "Man, that was a blast, and I don't think that I embarrassed myself."

Both nights, *The Dead* came on and did their extended set. With no chairs, people wandered around, danced, and sat in circles on the floor. Craze thought, "I can't believe that we just had this experience. It really IS what this business is all about…and our reward for all of the hard work."

Two weeks later the guys faced another huge crowd when they opened up for *Canned Heat*. *The Heat's* excellent musicianship blew the guys away but presented a huge problem. During *Canned Heat's* first set, Peter gathered the troops for a meeting back stage.

"Hey man, these guys are doing the same stuff that we play. These guys are so spectacular that we can't compete; they're beating us at our own game. We've got to rethink our whole approach. We can't play anything close to what they're doing. So we're gonna change gears and do a completely different set. It's our only chance of not getting blown off the stage."

In an attempt to contend with *The Heat's* professionalism, the guys humbly stepped into their shadow and changed their sets, making sure that nothing resembled *Canned Heat's* songs. Lawder later stated, "Simply put, these guys were the best band musically and professionally of the *Velvet Plastic* concerts."

Figure 14. *Canned Heat* and *Public Service* flyer.

Lawder's shiny black *Hagstrum* bass had taken one too many beatings. During the sound check for the *Canned Heat* concert and at the most inconvenient time, the bass guitar died. Lawder did everything he could to revive his old friend, but his bass had had enough. It just sputtered, crackled, and cut out. His amp refused the signal, and Lawder stood sadly over the dead instrument. Larry "The Mole" Taylor, bassist for *Canned Heat*, witnessed the whole thing. Understanding Lawder's sadness, The Mole walked over to Lawder and put his arm around him.

"Hey man too bad," he said. "I understand your pain. I'll tell you what, why don't you use my bass, It would be my honor."

Lawder replied, "Thanks man, I appreciate your offer.

Lawder put down the *Hagstrum* and strapped The Mole's *Fender Bass* around his neck. Lawder faced another dilemma: Lawder had gotten used to playing the thin-necked *Hagstrum*, but The Mole's *Fender bass's* neck was almost twice as wide as the *Hagstrum*. After two nights of fighting the wide-necked *Fender*, Lawder said, "Not only were my fingers killing me, but my forearms cramped so bad that they burned. By the second night, I really thought that I wasn't gonna be able to finish."

Soon after that experience, Lawder bought the same model bass guitar and has used it ever since. He said, "It took some doing, but I forced myself to learn the proper technique of playing a wider-necked guitar; the change actually made me a better bass guitar player...so, I can also thank The Mole for that introduction."

So the death of the *Hagstrum* did have some benefits. Switching to the wide-necked *Fender*, and hearing the superb musicianship of Larry "The Mole" Taylor, Lawder completely changed his style of playing the bass guitar.

Larry "The Mole" Taylor the bass guitar player; Robert "Bear" Hite the singer; "Fito" de la Parra, the drummer; and Henry "The Sunshine" Vestine all seemed like relatively normal guys. But one guy in *Canned Heat*, Allen "The Blind Owl" Wilson, seemed a little odd. Eyes described him as "stranger than fiction." The entire two days that the two bands hung out together, "The Blind Owl" wore a leather pilot's helmet with earflaps, chinstrap, and goggles. Most people would have taken off the helmet or at least raised the attached goggles; but not him. Craze thought, "He kind of wanders around, never saying anything to anybody. But his band seems to take this strange behavior in stride."

Besides the leather helmet, "The Blind Owl" did other bizarre things. After the first night's gig, and ready to leave the venue, both bands gathered in the lobby. Bear, the singer, said, "Wait a minute, where's The Owl; anybody seen the Owl?"

"The search was on"; both bands split up, and hunted for "The Owl." Frustrated, they gathered back in the lobby.

Bear said, "I want to go back to the hotel, but we can't leave him behind. He probably doesn't even know that he's in St. Louis."

Suddenly, like magic, "The Owl" appeared in the lobby door. Speaking for the first time in two days, "The Blind Owl" said, "What are you guys waiting for? Come on let's go."

The guys in *The Heat* shook their heads, and both bands left the premises.

A week before the next concert, *Jefferson Airplane*, Craze answered the phone. Eyes said, "Hey man, we're coming over."

Thinking nothing of it, Craze said, "Sure, I'll meet you guys out front."

Still wearing his cast, Craze met the guys outside as they pulled in front of his house. Peter, Lawder, and Eyes got out of the car and approached Craze sitting on the curb where years ago he made the lineups for his step ball games. Craze happily said, "Hey guys, what's up?"

Figure 14. Photo by Bill Meliick–courtesy of Dan Gaines. Pictures of Garcia the night we played with The Dead, and Eyes peeking out of curtain.

While Peter and Lawder stood staring at the ground, Eyes abruptly spoke up, "Hey man this just isn't working out. You're out man; it's over…"

After comprehending the impact of Eyes's words, Craze thought, "It's over. I'm out? Oh my God! It's over…It's ALL over."

Chapter 10

Tick, Tick, Tick

The three guys got in the van and drove off, leaving Craze standing on the curb where, years earlier, he had discovered music while playing step ball and chewing bubble gum. He watched as the van rounded the corner at the bottom of the tree-lined street and disappeared. Craze suddenly snapped back into reality by the unusual quietness of the almost always-busy neighborhood. The silence allowed his mind to wander back to that day when the music coming out of his neighbor's house rudely interrupting his game.

Craze walked across the street, up the steps of his terraced front yard, and down the short sidewalk leading to his porch. Climbing the three steps to the porch, Craze entered the front door of his usually bustling house. But for some reason, as if scripted, nobody was home.

With the TV left on by whoever watched it last, Craze sat on the empty couch thinking about what had just happened. Out of the corner of his eye, he noticed an episode of *The Three Stooges* on TV. Feeling isolated, he wasn't even interested in one of his favorite shows. But "the knuckleheads" and their shenanigans kept luring his eyes back to the TV. Paying more attention to the unavoidable distraction, Craze realized that in this episode, "Shemp" had replaced "Curly Joe." Craze suddenly understood the stories he had heard about "Curly" being crushed by his forced retirement. "Shemp" replaced "Curly," hampered by strokes, helped along by the beatings he took on the show.

Craze got up off the couch, and touching the screen as he passed by, he turned off the TV. From then on, Craze watched *The Three Stooges* with a new perspective.

𝄞

So Billy joined the band and Craze did the only thing he could do: get out of town. He and one of his few friends not related to the band took a six-thousand-mile journey out west and up into Canada. Later, Craze realized he did not remember much about this time. He returned from his trip not knowing anything about the band. For his own sanity, he did not want to know. Continuing to lose track of time, he thought, "Has it been three months… six months?"

His brain did not allow him to remember how long he had been banished from the band and exiled from his friends. Craze thought, "I don't know about this 'time heals all wounds' thing. Watching TV with the family isn't much of a replacement for my old life…Well, at least I can get out of bed now."

Taking one day at a time, Craze slowly learned how to put "one foot in front of the other" again and get on with his life.

𝄞

Eight-year-old Billy prepared for the exciting day that his parents had planned for the family. Billy continued his story to Craze, "As with most kids who lived in St. Louis, it didn't get any better than taking a boat ride on the Admiral!"

The excitement built as he walked up the ramp and entered the famous riverboat. While most of the other kids headed for the "game room" on the first deck, Billy had other plans. Having been on the riverboat before, Billy knew exactly where he wanted to go first: "I've got to see that ballroom."

Billy arrived at the 3rd floor ballroom as the boat dropped its moorings and began its trip down the mighty Mississippi. But before entering, he stopped and took a long look at the brand new Arch being built on the city's shoreline. Satisfied that he had seen enough, he entered the ballroom.

On stage, *The Lawrence Welk Orchestra* had begun their concert. Billy had seen them on TV many times, but for some reason, this time felt very different. He thought, "This sounds so different; I can hear everything so clearly."

Billy moved closer and ended up standing off to the side of the stage near the horn section. But most importantly, he had a perfect view of the captivating coordination of the hands and feet of the drummer. Up to this point in his life, nothing in the world had ever captivated him so deeply. He said to Craze, "The combination of seeing a live band performance for the first time and for some reason, instantly understanding how the whole thing worked changed my life forever."

One day while sitting in his room during that hazy period of time, Craze heard a knock at the front door. A few seconds later, Eyes, Peter, and Lawder entered his room. Eyes meekly asked, "How you doin' man? We heard you were back."

Craze replied, "Well okay I guess; what's up? What are you guys doing here?"

Slowly choosing his words, Eyes spoke up, "Man, this isn't working out. As far as gigs, we're doing well; but, without you, it's just not fun anymore. It isn't like it used to be. You brought us all together in the first place; you're like the glue or something. Without you here, it just isn't the same, man. Craze, we've talked it over and we want you back in the band."

Surprised, Craze's mind raced as he guardedly replied, "Man, I don't know. Don't get me wrong, there's nothing more that I'd rather do, but I can't EVER go through this pain again. You guys are great musicians; there was a reason you guys got rid of me. My arm is healed, but my limitations as a musician haven't changed.

"The fact remains that I'm not classically trained like Peter and Lawder. What you see is what you get—no more, no less. I need to know that you guys are SURE about what you're saying. I need to be guaranteed that the same thing won't EVER happen again. It would kill me to live through this nightmare again. For my own survival, history can't repeat itself."

As usual, Eyes spoke for all the guys, "We know we've hurt you, man and believe it or not, it hurt us too. We know now that the whole thing was a mistake, and you'll never know how sorry we are. We promise that you'll never have to worry about your place in the band again. We've learned our lesson."

Eyes continued, "Now hear me out; we have a plan. You know the profound affect that *The Canned Heat* had on all of us, and how we talked about becoming a full-fledged blues band. Well, let's do it...let's become a total blues band. And you're the perfect drummer for that job. You're a blues drummer and we know that now. The good of the band comes first, and we know you're the best man for this situation.

"Now, here's the real beauty of the plan. You know how good Billy is on the keyboard; well, he'll stay on as a second keyboard player. Think about all the other options we'll have. We'll have two fantastic keyboard players just like *The Allman Brothers*; just think about the possibilities!"

So Craze rejoined the new band, now known as *The Public Service Blues Band*. He thought, "Well sometimes I guess we get a second chance...but, do we really?"

Craze thought back to Billy's first encounter with the guys in the band. "Man, that introduction almost ended in disaster. As a matter of fact, somebody almost got hurt; and "somebody" meant Billy and his buddy.

The Public Service had contracted a gig at a local Catholic Church. The night of the church gig, everything went along just fine until suddenly, a guy in the front row started screaming at Lawder. Surprised by the interruption, Craze looked at the front row and saw two guys dressed in black trench coats with the collars up, and black, long, straight hair almost too-neatly cut. From behind his drums, Craze thought, "Why are these two guys wearing trench coats—it's the middle of the summer? And their hair-dos look like black helmets underneath those collars... what the heck is that one guy screaming about?"

Craze listened closer and when the guy finally screamed at the top of his lungs, Craze heard the words, "YOUR G'S FLAT. YOUR G'S FLAT."

"What the . . ."

Now, disrupting the show, the guy kept hollering the same words directly at Lawder. Craze noticed the Volcano brewing. Craze thought, "If this screaming keeps up, it's only a matter of time before the Volcano takes them out. God help this guy if he keeps screaming."

In the middle of a song, Lawder backed up along side Craze and leaned over screaming with red ears and flushed face, "You better figure out a way to shut that guy up or I'm gonna!"

Thankfully Eyes sensed the danger and signaled Craze to call for a break. After the song ended, Eyes and Craze corralled the Volcano and escorted him safely backstage. Lawder said, "Who is that guy, I'm gonna break that little SOB in half if I ever catch him; and what the hell was he shouting anyway?"

Craze thought as the Volcano slowly stopped fuming and the redness left his face, "Boy that was a close call."

Suddenly, Peter came walking backstage with the two strange little men in trench coats at his side. Spotting the unlikely trio, Craze thought, "Oh my god, it's the screamer and his clone."

With Lawder's back to Peter and the offenders, Eyes and Craze tried distracting Lawder, hoping the trench coat guys would turn around and leave.

But apparently totally unaware of the situation, Peter walked right up to the group with the two misfits in tow. Craze thought, "What is Peter thinking; doesn't he realize the danger? Didn't he see what was going down on stage?"

Obviously completely ignorant of the situation, Peter made things worse by getting Lawder's attention. Peter hollered, "Hey guys, I want to introduce you to my friend Billy and his friend, Richard Nickson."

Lawder turned around and immediately noticed the screamer and his sidekick. The Volcano immediately turned red, and flared up again. In an attempt to "save lives," Eyes and Craze feebly attempted to get between the Volcano and the troublemakers. Craze noticed Lawder's eyes widen, as the back of his hair lifted like a dog ready to attack. Then Billy spoke, "I'm so honored to finally meet you guys. I've been following you guys for a long time and I just love your music…and, by the way Lawder, YOUR G's FLAT."

For a second, the Volcano flared up again; but the calming affect of Billy's words doused the Volcano once and for all. With the Volcano now dormant, the conversation continued. Later, Lawder said, "By the way, my G was NOT flat."

This incident became the beginning of a life-long, close friendship.

Peter told Craze, "Did I tell you that Billy told me that he sleeps listening to a metronome? He said that he wanted to develop 'PERFECT METRONOME RECOGNITION.' He told me that people have to be BORN with perfect pitch, but he thought people can DEVELOP perfect time."

Craze thought, "Poor Billy can't help it. What a loving and strange guy; with all that music in his head getting in the way, he always seems…distracted."

From time to time, and without warning, Billy's brain would return to "music world," leaving him standing in a room with a blank look on his face. While in this mental state, when the guys spoke to him, Billy would literally pop up like a piece of popcorn, as he snapped back into reality. Then he would return to the conversation like nothing had just happened. Craze thought, "It's like his mind left the room for a while. It's just not fair, all those notes are stuck in his head and they keep getting in his way."

The band got used to dealing with the Volcano. But now they also had to contend with a "headless chicken." Lawder always wore the "task master" uniform in the band. But he did not hold a candle to Billy's insistence on perfection. Although Lawder agreed with Billy's doggedness, occasionally at rehearsal Lawder liked dialing in the "headless chicken act" just for fun. With a gleam in his eye, and before Billy arrived, Lawder gathered the guys together: "Hey tonight, I feel like having some fun. So let's push Billy's buttons, let's take turns making mistakes on purpose and see what Billy does. I know he'll go wild; just follow my lead."

On Lawder's cue, each guy took turns screwing up the rehearsed song. The guys eyed Billy as they waited for the "show to begin." After several mistakes, Billy took the bait and reacted. First, he jumped up from his keyboard and paced the floor. Then, holding his head like his "brains were falling out," Billy staggered around like "a chicken with his head cut off."

The "headless chicken" would then mumble, "I… I…can't stand it! I mean it; I'm serious…I can't stand it! What's wrong with you guys? You…you…know your parts, so what's the problem?"

Flopping around, staggering like a drunkard, still holding his head, and "serious as a heart attack," Billy continued, "What's wrong with you guys? We've rehearsed this song over and over; I demand satisfaction! Somebody explain this problem and I mean right now. I can't stand this sloppiness. I just don't get it! And you guys think you're professionals. Now, straighten up and get it right this time or else!"

With everybody quietly watching the "show," Lawder calmly answered, "Well Bill, we're sorry. I promise we'll get it right this time, won't we guys? Just settle down and take a seat and you'll see. We'll do better this time around; 'Cross my heart, hope to die.'"

𝄞

Before, during, and after his time in *The Public Service*, Billy had always considered Peter his quasi-mentor in both his musical and spiritual life. So Billy followed Peter's lead and attended Webster College, eventually earning a B. A. in Piano. He also followed in Lawder's steps by playing for a short time with another St. Louis evangelist, *The Reverend Cleophis Robinson* in St. Louis. By the mid-seventies, Billy signed a contract as a songwriter-producer with Berry Gordy's sister, Gwen, and was appointed musical director of her newly formed production company.

Throughout his days at *Motown* and later in his musical career, Billy worked with dozens of local and national icons. He continued working in the classical and blues fields but focused much of his efforts on grasping the anatomy of R and B. Billy confessed to Craze, "Over the years, I've maintained your ideology and the credo of *The Public Service*: 'You can't dig anybody until you dig yourself.'"

𝄞

Years later, Craze visited Eyes's house in L.A. Eyes called Billy and invited him to come over and visit. Billy answered: "Great, I'll be over at 1:00."

Eyes and Craze waited all day, and Billy never showed up. So Eyes and Craze figured that he had forgotten, which did not surprise them at all. The next day, at 1:00 sharp, the doorbell rang and there stood Billy at the front door. Not surprised by Billy's time mix-up Eyes said, "Billy, how you doing? Come on in."

Proud of himself, Billy answered, "Hey guys...looks like I'm right on time!" Eyes, Craze and Billy sat on the patio at Eyes's house in LA.

Eyes asked, "Hey Billy, you have any gigs coming up?" Billy answered with a concerned look on his face, "Yeah, tomorrow afternoon... outside.... around dark."

Eyes asked about the concerned look, "Well what's wrong man?"

Billy answered with a twisted face, and pretending to play the piano, "Well, you know man. That's when the bugs come out and get on the keys."

As Billy got ready to leave, he went to his car. At the same time, Eyes and Craze got in Eyes's pick-up truck to go to a *Dodgers* game. Eyes had started his truck when Billy appeared at Eyes's window. Eyes rolled his window and asked, "What's up man?"

Billy answered, "I think I left my keys in the house."

Eyes turned off the truck and handed Billy the keys. "Here and don't forget to lock the door."

Within a few seconds, Billy returned. "Can you help me man?"

Eyes got out of the truck, went inside and got Billy's keys. Eyes started the truck again when Billy knocked on the truck door one more time saying, "Sorry man, but I think I left my camera in the house. Can you help me out?"

Again, Eyes turned off the truck, handed Billy the keys, and said, "Okay, but this time, get it yourself."

A few minutes later, Billy walked around the corner with his camera, the tags still on it, mumbling, "I knew this thing would come in handy some day. Now, I just gotta figure out how to use it."

Raising his voice, Billy announced, "Everybody out...picture time..."

Needless to say, Eyes and Craze were late to the game.

𝄞

In his fifties and still playing music in L.A., Billy joined the TV and movie business as an extra, picking up a few bucks here and there. His most memorable part came when played the part of "William Shatner's hands playing the piano." Billy said, "Shatner asked me in typical intense 'Captain Kirk voice,' 'What do the pedals do?'"

𝄞

The Public Service Blues Band played for about one more year, but they had problems finding the spark of "the good old days." Eyes and Craze still preferred the raunchy sounds of the blues. With their formal training tugging at them, and pulling them in a completely different direction, Peter, Lawder, and Billy preferred much more complicated music. Rehearsals became a somewhat friendly battleground as both factions fought for supremacy of what songs were played and how they were performed.

Eyes admitted, "The gigs aren't as fun as they used to be; one side or the other always feels like the music lacks their input, and that situation drains the energy out of show. Lately, it feels like we're just going through the motions."

The "piss and vinegar" of their youthful unanimity had gone by the wayside. Besides the band's musical tastes going in different directions, Eyes already attended college and the rest of the guys planned on going to college that fall. So *The Public Service Blues Band* faced the inevitable fact that "all bands will die."

But the guys in the band wanted their band to die with dignity. College became the perfect excuse for breaking up and settling the unrest peacefully. Still concerned about each other's welfare, the guys made a pact: "Before we make an official break-up, we'll continue playing gigs together until all members have joined other bands."

So *The Public Service Blues Band* slowly faded away. After all members became part of new bands, the band officially broke up. The classy break-up showed the commitment that they still had for each other...and this commitment to each other's welfare never went away. But for now, they went their separate musical ways.

𝄞

KSHE radio, the first "progressive" FM radio station in St. Louis, had just gone on air. Craze joined a band created for promoting the new station called *Prince Knight's Old Fashioned Rock and Roll Boogie Band*. The band played in front of big crowds at the higher-end clubs and large outside events promoting *KSHE*... and made a lot of money. At several events *Prince Knight*, a DJ at the station, would jump on stage, give his "station promotion" speech, then "fake play" the trumpet with the band. Craze thought, "Prince has no idea how to play, but he DOES have a trumpet! So we'll go along with his stunt...after all, Prince signs the checks."

Among others, *The Boogie Band* consisted of two older dudes named Cooley and Duffy. Growing up and living in the inner city, Cooley and Duffy had played the blues in the area for years. Craze thought, "Cooley and Duffy are scruffy; but they're good people. They're biker-type guys who dress like 'gang bikers' but can't afford the bikes. Playing in this band is like playing the blues on the dark side of the moon. I feel like I've gone from 'spit shine and polish' and straight into the gutter. We had one rehearsal before Cooley (the leader) had us off and running. Even simple blues numbers like the songs that they play need more practice than this."

As the band put the "sloppy" show on the road, a disappointed Craze thought about himself, "Boy, what people will do to make money! I'm actually embarrassed being seen playing with this band. Are their crowds deaf? Why would anybody want to hear this crap?"

But Craze had to admit, "It IS fun playing with Cooley and Duffy."

One night while doing an event at a local club for *KSHE*, *The Boogie Band* opened up for *The Spencer Davis Group,* a popular British Invasion rock band. Craze's new band played their usual sloppy set and got off stage. During breaks, Cooley asked Craze, "Hey man, can Duffy and me borrow your car keys?"

This ritual had become a normal event during breaks. So Craze, with motorcycles out of his life, handed over the keys to his eight-year-old, 1962 Chevy convertible. Cooley graciously said, "Thanks man," and the two headed outside.

The first couple of times the guys asked for the keys, Craze worried, "What the heck are those two doing in my car? Whatever it is, I hope it's legal."

So during one break, Craze handed over his keys, waited a few minutes, and then headed out to his well-kept car. Walking up from behind the car, Craze heard Cooley talking, "Hey Duff, just smell that."

Duffy replied, "Yeah man isn't this great!"

Craze thought, "Uh, oh…" He came around the side of the car and saw the two old biker types sitting in the back seat taking deep breaths, sniffing and smelling. Craze knocked on the back window and as Cooley rolled the window down, Cooley said, "What's up man?"

Craze asked, "What are you guys up to?"

Cooley answered, "Man this is so cool; we've never driven in a new car before. We just love that 'new car smell.' We've never smelled it before."

From then on, Craze happily handed over the keys so Cooley and Duffy could go suck in the smell of his new car. Craze thought, "Whatever 'makes your boat float'; if it makes those guys happy, what the heck. Besides, it's cheap AND legal entertainment."

The Boogie Band returned inside, just in time to catch the *Spencer Davis* set. With the lights down so low, they had difficulty observing the movements onstage. Craze thought, "I'm having flashbacks to the night that we first saw *The Allman Joy*."

Suddenly a spotlight hit the bass player. Wearing shiny turquoise pants and a shiny bright orange shirt, he began the song *"Gimme Some Lovin'."* The shocked crowd hardly had time to respond before a second spotlight fired-up on the *Hammond* organ playing it's powerful intro to the song. Then full lights, and the whole band joined in. After the first song, and without hesitation, the room went dark again and the band started into *"I'm a Man* (yes I am and I can't help but love you so)." The spotlight hit the bass player's intro, but this time, the second spotlight focused on the drummer's beginning part. Finally, with full lights on, the rest of the band again joined in.

Witnessing one of the best intros he had ever experienced, Craze thought, "That's what I call great intros! The band hit the audience 'right between the eyes,' got them excited, and didn't let go. You can begin shows several different ways, but, this one really did the job. They got the crowd's attention and left them begging for more."

The Spencer Davis Group played a great show that night, and Craze never forgot seeing one of the best openings he had ever witnessed.

Craze could not wait to tell Eyes and Ralph (one of their old equipment managers) about the *Spencer Davis* show. The guys in the now-defunct *Public Service Blues Band* kept in touch by meeting in various food establishments after their gigs. So on this occasion, the three met up at a local pizza joint near the office

CHAPTER 10

Figure 16. *Boogie Band* business card.

of *Velvet Plastic Productions*. Craze entered the pizza joint where the other two guys had already grabbed a table near the front door. Eyes had on an American flag vest, which he often wore to his gigs. As Craze sat down, he noticed some older guys in suits sitting in the back of the restaurant. While they ordered, Craze patiently waited to tell his story.

All of a sudden, Craze felt a punch to the face. As he fell to the floor, a big guy in a suit with a gun strapped inside his coat stood over him. The suited-guy hollered in Craze's face, "POLICE; DON'T MOVE!"

Craze watched from the floor as other suited guys dragged Eyes out the front door. They hauled him to the gutter and began beating him up. Craze could hear Eyes screaming, "Please stop, I can't see who you are without my glasses."

Craze saw Eyes's glasses sitting in the gutter next to the American flag vest. He heard one of the suit-guys say something about desecrating the flag. Finally, one of the suited guys handcuffed Eyes and threw him in the back seat of an unmarked car. The guy holding Craze down got up, walked away, got into the car with Eyes and drove off.

Worried about Eyes and dazed by the blow and this insane event, Craze got up and rubbed his punched cheek. A couple seconds later, Ralph walked in the front door and said, "Let's get out of here. I'll explain later; meet me at Eyes's house."

They both got in their cars and sped off. Craze arrived just as Ralph closed his trunk and tucked something under his arm. He also carried Eyes's glasses in one hand. They banged on the door, waking up Eyes's parents and explained the situation. Eyes's dad called the police. When he hung up he announced, "They've arrested Eyes for 'desecrating the flag.'"

Ralph spoke up next, producing the flag vest, "Well, I need to show you what I have. When they knocked me down outside the restaurant, I fell right on top of the vest and Eyes's glasses. Nobody paid any attention, so I got up, ran to my car, and threw the vest in my trunk...I'm sure nobody saw me."

Eyes's dad said, "Well, I think I need to take possession of that thing. Guys, let's not mention this to anybody else." Ralph and Craze agreed.

Craze attended court for Eyes's preliminary hearing. As he sat in the audience, the prosecutor announced, "Mister Eyes is being tried for desecrating the flag."

The judge asked, "Will the prosecutor please present the evidence?"

"Judge, that might be a problem...Somehow, we've misplaced the article of clothing."

The judge responded, "Well that IS a problem. Will the lawyers please approach the bench?"

After a short discussion, everybody returned to his seat. The judge announced,

"The defendant has agreed to plead guilty to the misdemeanor charge of 'disturbing the peace,' three years suspended sentence, and no record. Court adjourned."

After leaving court, Eyes's dad explained, "The lawyer suggested that we take the plea because fighting this thing might drag out for a long time and cost a lot of money. So Eyes and I decided to get this thing over with once and for all."

As it turned out, not only did Cooley and Duffy play with *The Boogie Band,* they also played for the famous icon *Chuck Berry,* as his St. Louis back-up band. When Craze joined Cooley and Duffy, Craze became Chuck's St. Louis drummer, a perk that Craze did not know about when he joined *The Boogie Band.* By that time in his career, Chuck did not travel with a band. He used different local musicians as his back-up band in all the different cities where he played. So when Chuck played in St. Louis, Cooley and Duffy provided his back-up band.

Chuck played regularly at his "pool/park", named *Berry Park,* located just outside the city of St. Louis. Pool/parks and drive-in movies were a popular outdoor family activity in the Midwest. For a fee, a family could enter the park, grab a picnic table in the park, and spend the day picnicking and swimming. Craze thought of pool/parks as sort of drive-ins on steroids. For a small amount of money, a family could enjoy either wholesome pastime. In the case of pool/parks the activity lasted all day instead of just an evening at a drive-in. MAKE NO MISTAKE, Craze loved both.

At the time, most pool/parks and drive-ins were segregated, so blacks did not have the luxury of participating in either activity. *Chuck Berry* decided that he wanted an integrated pool/park, so he bought land and built his own integrated park. The guitar-shaped pool became world famous because of its unique shape. He also built his house and a nightclub in the pool area. He used the nightclub to attract more business. The patrons realized that live entertainment came with the package, but "you never know, *Chuck Berry* himself might show up and play."

Cooley called Craze and asked, "Hey man, you mind drivin' to *Berry Park* this time? You know, we really like bein' in your car."

Craze thought, "Well they'll help pay for the gas…and by the way, AIR IS FREE." So with Cooley and Duffy sitting in the back seat, and sucking in the "new car" air, Craze chauffeured his two new buddies to *Berry Park*.

On the way to Craze's first gig with Chuck, Cooley spoke up. "Now Craze there are certain things you need to know when you play with Chuck. If you pay attention to these rules, you'll do fine.

"First of all, we'll spend the whole day because Chuck may play at any time. So when he decides it's time to go on stage, be ready; so whatever you do, don't leave the park.

"Remember *Chuck Berry* is THE SHOW, so keep it simple, lay-back, and don't EVER UPSTAGE HIM. Here's the most important thing to remember: No matter where you are in the park, do NOT say anything about Chuck. Word has it that Chuck's a little paranoid and we think that he's got the place wired. Apparently Chuck can watch or listen to you anywhere in the park. We think he has a set-up in his bedroom where he can spy on everybody. So keep your mouth shut." Craze took the information to heart.

Craze felt excited as he entered the park. He thought, "Man, what a great honor. My next adventure: I'm gonna be playing with a legend. This gig should be really cool."

Craze witnessed the famous guitar-shaped pool for the first time. The neck of the guitar-pool aimed at Chuck's club, while the body end of the pool faced Chuck's house. Both low profile structures were built in the fifties, ranch-style architecture. People swam in the pool and picnicked in the park.

The great *Chuck Berry* met the band at the front door of his house saying, "Welcome gentlemen, I'll open the club so you can set up."

He looked at Craze and said, "Hi, I'm *Chuck Berry*." Craze shook his hand and replied, "Nice to meet you, I'm Craze."

As they walked across the pool patio to the club, Chuck's two kids, a boy around the age of ten and a girl around the age of twelve, tagged along. Chuck's son carried Chuck's guitar case. As Chuck unlocked the door, he noticed that the boy had set his guitar down and started walking away. Chuck looked at his son and said, "Hey boy, that's our living; don't ever leave that guitar unattended. Now show that guitar some respect, and pick it up."

Craze thought, "I've only been here a couple of minutes, and he's already made a profound statement."

Being a gracious host, Chuck made the band feel quite comfortable in the pleasant surroundings. Chuck usually stayed in the house and kept to himself, while Craze spent most of his time on a private patio playing chess with Chuck's two kids. When it came time to play, the band followed Chuck out of his house, with one of the kids carrying his guitar, across the pool-patio, and to the small, clean, club. As Cooley, Duffy, and Chuck tuned up, the crowd flowed in. Then without warning, Chuck played the first song, leaving the band to figure out exactly what song he had started. He did not announce the song or count it down; he just started playing. At first, Craze rationalized, "Well everybody knows *Chuck Berry's* tunes, so what the heck; this should be a piece of cake."

Craze easily followed iconic rock-n-roll tunes like *"Johnny B Good"* and *"Route 66."* But Chuck's ballads became a completely different story. Craze thought, "I can improvise as good as the next guy, but Chuck just starts playing a solo; no tempo or indication of what song he's playing whatsoever."

The three band members struggled for several bars, until they eventually picked up the rhythm and timing of the ballad, which made the beginnings of those songs pretty rough. Craze remembered, "Those ballads never got any easier."

The first time they played *"Johnny B Good,"* Craze felt confident playing the song, so to add a little spice, he did a drum roll. Chuck turned back, gave Craze the stink eye, and shook his head, "NO," as if he were saying, "Don't show me up, I'm the star here."

Craze thought, "Oops, I think I just broke the 'number one rule.' DON'T EVER UPSTAGE CHUCK!"

Chuck had a unique approach to his music: He played his songs exactly the same way, with exactly the same equipment as the day that the songs were written. He left the music "pure," untouched, and raw. So his songs sounded exactly the same as the day that they were written, no-frills, rustic "Rock-a Billy."

Craze thought, "Some people might call this approach an asset. I understand some of it, but he also hasn't added ANY modern technology like an updated sound system. There's a reason new sound systems were invented, and in my opinion, an updated sound system doesn't alter the overall affect; it just makes it easier for the audience to hear what he's doing. As a matter of fact, sometimes he can't even hear what's going on, and he misses the beat. Almost all other fifties icons like *Jerry Lee Lewis, Little Richard*, and *Elvis* bolstered their sound systems, which improved the audience's experience, but NOT CHUCK BERRY…with Chuck, 'What you see is what you get,' raw, basic, and nothing improved."

Years later, Chuck's daughter Gwen sang lead in her own band. All grown up, her locally-popular band played in Craze's new home of Columbia, Missouri. Craze attended the show and after the gig, he introduced himself to Gwen. He told her the story about playing with her dad at *Berry Park*. Happy to hear the story, Gwen invited Craze to a party after the gig. Craze and

Gwen had a great time spending the evening telling "Chuck" stories.

Craze mentioned, "Hey Gwen, do you remember me at all?"

She did not remember Craze since so many musicians played with her dad over the years. Craze said, "Well believe it or not, I spent my time at *Berry Park* playing chess with you and your brother on the back patio."

She replied, "Wow, my brother and I did spend summers playing chess on our patio. That's very cool."

Throughout the evening, they traded stories. At one point, Gwen said, "I've got one for you. A few years ago, my dad decided that he needed female back-up singers. I guess he got the idea from *Ike and Tina Turner's Ikettes*. So he asked me to be one of his singers. On the tour, we played a gig *The Hollywood Bowl* in L.A.

"I saw a long-haired, scraggly guy jump on stage and start wailing on his guitar. From my vantage point, I couldn't get a good look at the guy. All of a sudden, my dad walked over to the security guard and had the guy thrown off stage. The next day I read a headline in a local newspaper, 'Chuck Berry throws Keith Richards of *The Rolling Stones* off stage at the *Hollywood Bowl*.' I asked my dad, 'Didn't you know who he was? Why would you throw one of the most famous musicians in the world off stage?'

He answered, "I don't know about any *Rolling Stones* or whatever they call themselves. It's my show and who did this Keith Richards think he was coming on my stage and trying to take over my act.'"

𝄞

Later on, Chuck and Keith must have made up, because Keith made a documentary about Chuck called "*Hail, Hail, Rock and Roll.*" In it, Chuck constantly argued with Keith, insisting on doing things his way. Keith tried to save Chuck and his legacy from his years of sloppy performances, but Chuck did not make the process easy on Keith. While watching the documentary, Craze felt Keith's pain having lived through the some of the same experiences while playing with *The Great Chuck Berry*.

Craze saw *Chuck Berry* play one more time at a street concert in Columbia. Chuck played his usual sloppy show, packed up his Cadillac—located directly behind the stage—collected his money, and got out of town before the audience had a chance to request an encore.

𝄞

Craze thought of words to an *Animals* song, "We've got to get out of this place, if it's the last thing we ever do…"

During his final semester at a St. Louis junior college and feeling more stagnant by the minute, Craze sat in the student cafeteria looking around. He felt tired; tired of big city life, tired of playing bad music, and tired of girls everywhere but no one to take out.

He thought, "'Water, water everywhere, and not a drop to drink.' I feel like I have nothing to offer to girls. They don't want to date a burned out and depressed 'old has –been.' I'm certainly not gonna take them to a *Boogie Band* gig; I'm too embarrassed. It's time to pick myself up, and get out of the gutter. It's time to get a new life."

Chapter 11

Moving on and Out

Craze looked forward to life in the college town of Columbia, Missouri. He set up camp in a basement apartment on campus with two friends from Webster Groves. He thought, "Freedom at last; I'm on my own for the first time and I love it. Now it's time to find a job and make this move successful."

On his first day in his new apartment, after walking a short two blocks, he came to a local restaurant/bar with a sign reading "Help Wanted." He walked in, applied, and immediately got the job. "Well, so far so good," he thought. "Things are falling right into place."

Little did he know how profound that statement would turn out to be.

As he sat at the bar after the interview, he struck up a conversation with another guy sitting at the bar. The guy leaned over to Craze and said, "Hi I'm Jesse…you new in town?"

"Yeah, I just moved here yesterday."

"Where you from?"

"Webster Groves."

"Hey, I know people from Webster; some are musicians. You play?"

"Yeah, I'm a drummer."

"I play too, man, I sing and play guitar. Maybe we can get together some time and play."

"Cool man, I'm up for it. Here's my number, just give me a call any time."

As the conversation went on, Craze thought, "This guy's voice sings even when he talks. It's almost angelic; I've never heard anything like it."

Jesse then said, "Since you're from the St. Louis area, have you ever heard of *Velvet Plastic Productions*?" That got Craze's attention.

"Yeah man, we did several concerts for them."

"Well, maybe you've heard of my old band, *The Sound Farm*? A couple of years ago we opened-up for *Albert King* at the *Velvet Plastic Ball*."

Figure 17. "VP" Ball, *Albert King* and *Sound Farm*.

CHAPTER 11

Craze thought back to that night at *The Ball* remembering an almost operatic voice coming off the stage and thinking that he had never heard such powerful vocals. "You bet! I was there and I remember your vocals. Your VOICE is what I remember. Man, you can sing!"

"Thanks man, that night was very cool."

Craze thought, "I've been in town for a day, got a job and made a contact in the music scene with one of the most outstanding voices that I've ever heard. This move is working out just fine."

Craze got that call from Jesse.

"Hey man, it's Jesse. I've got a keyboard player who wants to jam with us. You might know him. He's Joey from Webster. He says he knows you."

"Wow man, that's cool. I've known Joey since I was six. We used to go to church together; let's do it."

"Great, by the way, do you know any bass guitar players? I'm having a hard time finding one."

"Let me think about it." Craze sat in his living room thinking out loud.

"Man, I don't know any bass players around here. Hey Wayne, you know any bass players?" His roommate looked at Craze like he was nuts.

"Man, you just made my mind puke. I'm a bass player you idiot!"

Realizing that Wayne had a bass guitar sitting in his room and that Craze had actually heard him play several times, AND after the redness left his face, Craze thought, "Oh, I guess I forgot. Well anyway, problem solved, I found our bass player."

So Jesse replaced his time in the now-defunct *Sound Farm* with devoting his time to *The Hard Corps*; and Jesse's Midwest fame followed him to this new band. Besides his voice, and some of his own original tunes, Jesse brought along several other original songs written by his old bandmate and close friend Bear. Bear's songs had already had a profound affect on the Mid-Missouri audiences, so by putting "different spins" on Bear's music, *The Hard Corps* had plenty of originals. With only a couple rehearsals under their belts, Jesse announced that he had booked some dates. Craze freaked out and thought, "Here we go again. Man, I hope this band doesn't turn out to be another *The Boogie Band*. I ain't going through that nightmare again."

Obviously Jesse drove this bus. So for the moment, Craze went along with the plan. Although, the music suffered now and then from lack of rehearsal time, most of the time Jesse's combination of killer original music, show tunes and classic country standards bloomed into beautiful works of art. He used the stage as a kind of laboratory, changing rhythms and tempos on the spot. On stage, songs evolved on the fly, taking new directions as they were performed.

Craze thought, "It takes a little while getting used to doing things this way, but so far, it's working out just fine. The improvised music is a little rough at first, and I can live with it as long as we end up with positive results.

"I've never witnessed 'show tunes' played in rock form before, and the original songs are killer; and let's not forget that voice...that unbelievable voice. This guy can blow audiences away at will."

The guys soon learned the key to playing with Jesse when he introduced new, unrehearsed material on stage: "FOLLOW JESSE'S CUES." For months, the band broke into the climax of a tune as Jesse broke out his secret weapon: "THE NOTE." He reached for the sky and hit the unbelievably high D note above high C. At first, the note struck audiences silent; then, a second or two later as the crowd realized what they had just witnessed, it sent them into orbit, screaming and cheering. For months, turning Jesse loose worked wonders on the adoring crowds. But then, things got strange.

In the meantime, Jesse announced the band's latest gig: opening up for *The Ozark Mountain Daredevils* in Springfield, Missouri.

CHAPTER 11

At a time when most bands got more complicated using synthesizers and other electronic devices, *The Daredevils* took a different approach. They kept their country-rock music uncomplicated and laid-back. The band let their lyrics and down-to-earth-melodies become their weapon. *The Daredevils'* power came from simplicity. No one dominated the stage or stood out from the rest of the other guys in the band. Craze thought, "Man, this 'keep it simple' approach makes their music so tight. It's hard to discern the individual sounds of each instrument when they're playing. All the instruments bond into one forceful sound."

Craze remembered a conversation with Randy, the creator of *The Ozark Mountain Daredevils*. He told Craze that he used *Buffalo Springfield* as a blueprint in forming the group: "I gathered writers together and didn't necessarily worry about their musicianship. We'd worry about that problem later."

So each member in his band wrote songs, very good songs, giving them massive amounts of material. The matter of "who played what instrument" took care of itself in due time. His unique approach demonstrated an extremely successful venture: five gold albums proved Randy's point.

The Daredevils' recent debut album and their single *"If You Want to Get to Heaven"* rocketed the band to celebrity status. Soon after the concert that Craze and his band had attended, *The Daredevils'* manager, Paul, had an idea:

"Why don't you guys put together the old *Sound Farm* and perform at our 'Coming Home' concert in Springfield, Missouri. *The Sound Farm* had a tremendous influence on most of the guys in *The Dares*, including me. I think it's a perfect match."

So Craze's band took Paul's advice and added two former members from *The Sound Farm*, Bear and John. Craze liked the idea that his participation, although nobody but he and Supe knew it, represented *The Public Service's* influence on Supe also. After a few practices, far too little in Craze's opinion, the revised version of *The Sound Farm* departed for Springfield.

The event took place in an old theater in downtown Springfield. Backstage before the concert, the two bands buzzed with anticipation as they prepared themselves for their performances. Taking in the ambiance of the old structure, Craze thought, "This is the perfect venue for this happening. Here we are honoring our old friends in this perfect setting. This should be fun."

Little did he know how wrong that statement would become... events did not turn out quite the way Craze had expected.

Introduced as a major influence on the *Daredevils* music, *The Sound Farm* went on stage first and began their set. Immediately things just didn't feel right to Craze. He thought, "We may be playing the same songs but with Bear and John playing, there's two different interpretations of the same music. It's like we're playing two completely different songs at the same time."

As the set continued, Craze thought, "I'm getting pulled in two different directions; my job as the drummer is to hold this thing together. Instead, it's like driving a car with one wheel not connected to the steering wheel. With so many strong personalities on stage and nobody giving in, this thing is getting real painful. We just didn't rehearse enough."

The situation got more and more out-of-hand as the band struggled through their set. Finally, they ended their set with a beautiful song written by Bear. The song contained a critical time change from 4/4 to 6/8. At the same moment that the time change came, Bear looked at Craze and shook his head, "NO." Without time to react, Craze played through the time change. Craze crashed the out-of-control car, blowing the climatic ending of the song. Instead of bringing the house down, the song and the set ended in a fizzle. Dumbfounded by the mistake, Craze thought about the incident, "But Bear shook off the break! I just followed the guy who wrote the song."

Later, Craze played several more gigs with Bear. After observing Bear's mannerisms on stage, Craze realized that Bear ALWAYS shook his head "NO." Craze thought, "It's just Bear's way of expressing his passion for the song. It's not a signal at all. It's a good idea to know the people you play with before you get on stage with them. My mistake..."

After the rough set and blown finale, Craze couldn't face the crowd. The rest of the band went out in the audience and listened to *The Dares* while Craze looked for someplace to hide. He found some stairs backstage that led to the basement. The old but clean basement became the perfect place for Craze to lick his wounds and hide.

The Dares started playing above his head. Craze walked around and listened to the music above. While roaming around, he found a small door about waist high and four feet tall. Craze opened the small door and realized that he had discovered the dirt-floored space under the stage. He climbed in, lay on his back and closed the door. In the pitch-black space, Craze could hear the band perfectly. Being literally underneath the band, he could also hear each member tapping his feet. This new dimension of listening to a live band intrigued Craze.

"I can hear each individual foot-tap. Each member is creating the syncopation they need to play their part. It's all in perfect time, yet every foot-tap has a different accent. Is that Randy at lead guitar? That must be John, the rhythm guitar player, and so on. What a great way to listen to a band."

After the concert, Craze crawled out of the space, brushed himself off and joined the other band members backstage.

Craze knew that the band had a place to stay after the concert, but he had no idea where. Craze and company followed *The Daredevils* for "what seemed like forever" out in the country to a place called The Ruedi (pronounced Rudy) Valley Ranch.

Some of *The Dares* had rented the old southern mansion located in a beautiful valley. The bands arrived and approached the house. A large old porch greeted them. Entering the old estate, they noticed that each of the sizeable rooms of the old mansion contained a fireplace large enough to stand in. Fires burned in some of the fireplaces creating a warm, welcoming environment. The large porch, sizeable rooms and lots of land provided plenty of room for the bands to roam. The dining room had a huge table filled at all times with food and drink.

As the weekend progressed, Craze thought, "I had no idea how cool that this place would be, and this table set-up is the icing on the cake; it reminds me of a Viking feast. But the best part of this weekend is the music. No matter where you go, the porch, every room and every location on this ranch has music playing. Everybody finds their spot and joins together in song. This get-together is a once-in-a-lifetime event."

Craze might have been disappointed by his performance at the show, but his fond memories of The Ruedi Valley Ranch more than made up for the bad experience.

𝄞

Years later after Randy had left the band, Craze asked him if he ever regretted leaving *The Ozark Mountain Daredevils*. Randy replied, "Every morning when I wake up, my first thought is that I'm no longer a member of *The Dares*."

Craze thought about that profound statement. "Leaving a band is like getting a divorce. You still love them but you know it's over and there's not a damn thing you can do about it."

𝄞

One night as the band set up a perfectly timed climax of a song, they prepared themselves for the show-stopping note and the following crowd eruption. Jesse approached the microphone and busted into a…GUITAR SOLO. The balloon popped, the energy in the room vanished. Never in his whole life, had Craze ever witnessed such self-inflicted destruction on stage. Craze thought, "Man, what is he doing?"

From then on, "the note" got used less and less, while more and more guitar solos filled the void. Because of Jesse's overwhelming control over the band, the guys in the band never had the guts to mention this huge debacle. Craze thought, "Jesse's intentionally ignoring the gift that God gave him and replacing his 'gift' with guitar leads. I don't get it! Anybody else on the planet would be ecstatic to have such a talent. But he's annihilating his gift by using metal strings instead of his vocal chords… and apparently on purpose. People come to hear that voice, and he's denying them his gift; to me, that denial is almost sinful. I guess he's trying to invent a new gift, but it ain't working."

The *faux pas* happened more and more and finally completely took over. Jesse's band gave up on him and his cause. Craze, Joey, and Wayne quit because they could no longer tolerate such a blunder with one of God's perfect gifts.

Years later, as Craze and Joey sat in Joe's mom's kitchen in St. Louis talking about old times, Joey simply stated, "Why did Jesse do that?"

Craze knew exactly what Joey meant by the question, but neither answered. They both sat and pondered the unanswerable question. Craze finally answered, "I don't know man."

They both knew that the question would remain a mystery to them forever.

𝄞

Craze stood behind his newly purchased congas, one black and one white, anxiously awaiting the first song of his new career as a conga player. He had affectionately named them "George and Dolores" after his mom and dad. Selling his beloved Ludwig drum set and buying the congas had been a difficult choice. But a long talk with his dad about "leaving the past behind and moving on when an opportunity presents itself" had helped him make the decision. Alongside him stood bass player Wayne from *The Hard Corps*, a hot alto sax player named T-Mac, and "Tookie," the leader of the band.

Craze thought, "I feel almost naked standing up here without a drum set; there's nowhere to hide."

Tookie played an acoustic guitar as he directed the band through his sometimes tricky, sometimes extremely fast music. As Craze followed Tookie's lead, Craze thought, "How would I describe this music…maybe up-tempo jazz/folk/rock, if there is such a thing? Tookie's style reminds me of *Jesse Colon Young* and his band *The Young Bloods*. Well whatever it's called, I love playing it.

"But what I love most about playing with Took: I can read his musical-mind like a book. It's like our brains are connected; I instinctively know what this guy's gonna do next in a song. I know where he's going before he does it."

Craze had recently opened a stained glass studio. At night, he played great music with Tookie and the band; during the day, he built stained glass windows. The studio, located in an old lumberyard warehouse converted into studios, provided a great view overlooking the downtown area. Because of the central location, the studio became a perfect meeting place. When passing through the area, fellow musician friends like *Supe Granda* and other members of *The Ozark Mountain Daredevils* often stopped by and paid Craze a visit.

On this particular night, the band played at what they considered their home base, a luxurious lounge located in one of the upscale restaurants in town. Coincidentally, Craze's stained glass studio had been hired to build windows for all the exterior windows. So as the band played on the roomy stage at the end of the room, Craze looked over the plush leather couches and chairs filled with people digging their low key, yet wild music, AND his newest stained glass window.

"Man, this is living," he thought. "I'm playing great music in a great place, filled with great people, and beautiful black-gowned waitresses all over the place. And besides that, I get to look at my latest stained glass window. I feel like I'm living in a Ronald Reagan B-type movie where everything is perfect. I'm having the time of my life…I hope this dream goes on forever."

Craze thought about T-Mac, the sax player: "If I'd draw a picture of what I thought a beatnik looked like, the picture would look exactly like T-Mac. This guy can't stop moving while he's performing. He's literally 'effervescent' on stage. He puts his feelings into his instrument more than anybody that I've ever met, except for maybe Duane Allman. Like Duane, T-Mac's instrument becomes part of his body and soul while he's up there."

T-Mac had just gotten married and had a kid. On the afternoon of one gig, he and his wife got into a horrible fight, and she threw him out. Arriving on the scene and discovering T-Mac's condition, Craze thought, "This guy's a mess. Is Took going to let him play or send him home?"

After talking to T-Mac, Tookie came over to Wayne and Craze and said, "He says he's all right, so I guess we'll see what happens."

Prepared for the worst, the guys started the show. Craze thought, "This could turn into a disaster real quick. Well, as they say the show must go on, so let's give this a shot."

Tookie started the first song. But to their surprise, the most melancholy sounds that the guys had ever heard came out of T-Mac's horn. After that initial surprise, no matter what song they played, fast or slow, happy or sad, the whole set turned into the saddest most beautiful sounds that the band had ever heard. Craze saw women wiping their eyes in the awestruck audience.

Craze thought, "How does he do that?" I've never seen anything like it. He single-handedly changed every song we played into his personal feelings…amazing." Craze had always preached, "When a musician walks on stage, he must leave the bad day on the bottom step. Remember, the audience paid their hard-earned money to see your best. They could be doing a million other things, but they decided to come and see you. So give them the best you've got and leave the bad mood behind. But in this case, T-Mac proved me wrong."

During the break, Wayne and Craze sat on the side of the stage, astonished by what they had just witnessed. Wayne looked at Craze and said, "You know Craze, most people spend their entire lives trying to put their feelings into their music, and this guy can't help it."

𝄞

After this experience with T-Mac, Craze had an epiphany. He finally realized the difference between Duane Allman's "inner soul" charisma and Eyes's "always aware of the audience" charm. They both had "IT," but their attraction to the masses came from completely different places in their hearts.

𝄞

For over a year after graduating from college, Craze lived the "Life of Riley," playing great music and making stained glass windows. One afternoon in his studio, Craze busied himself working on his latest creation. Tookie walked in as he had done so many times before. But this time, he had a stern expression on his face. Ignoring the look, Craze as usual looked up from his work and asked, "What's up man?"

"Hey man, I might as well cut to the chase. I'm leaving the band and starting up a southern rock band with my brother. Sorry man, but I have to make this move."

"I guess you've already made up your mind, and there's no talking you out of this decision?"

"No man, it's over!"

"Well, like they say, blood's thicker than water."

Craze had now heard the words "it's over" one more time. Although Tookie made the death of the band swift, Craze still felt the sting. As Tookie left the studio, Craze looked out the window at the view of downtown. The conversation and the band were terminated. Craze suddenly thought, "I'm a sideman, and I always will be. My job is to make the guy standing in front of me on stage look good, and I'll always be at the mercy of that person. My dreams always vaporize because of somebody else's whim, and I can't do anything about it. Still, I just can't face starting over again."

Starting over one more time and leaving destiny in the hands of someone else one more time became an insurmountable obstacle. Craze knew in his heart that his band-playing days had just come to an end.

𝄞

Perched safely in his stained glass studio and away from the cold-cruel world of bands, Craze worked on building stained glass windows for a historical railroad station turned into a restaurant. Still licking his wounds from the break-up that had happened only one month earlier, his landlord, Pete entered the studio, and said, "Craze, how you doing? Do you have a second? I've got something I'd like to toss at you."

"Sure Pete, come on in and make yourself comfortable. What's on your mind?"

"Well, I've done some checking around town, and I've heard people refer to you as 'the hippie businessman.' They say that you are the perfect man for a project that I have in mind. Of course you know that I own *Ford's Theater* (the largest bar in town), and I'm planning on making major changes in my bar.

"You know that it's a DJ bar right now, but I'd like to make some major modifications; I want to change the bar into a live entertainment venue, and that will take some expertise. Craze, I think you're the best man for the job, so I'd like to offer you a job as the bar's Entertainment Manager.

"First of all, you'd be in charge of converting the interior of the bar into a live entertainment venue. Then, after those changes are made, you'd be responsible for all the entertainment bookings. In both cases, I'd turn you loose; you'd be in charge, and you would make all the decisions."

Craze thought for a moment, "Man, I just swore off the band business, and now this happens."

"Well Pete, I don't know, I just got out of that business, and I promised myself that I'd stay away."

Pete said, "Craze, tell me what it would take to change your mind. I've done my homework, and I've decided that I want you for the job."

Craze quickly put together his thoughts and said, "First of all, I guess I'd need a percentage of the business for my own protection; then I'd need a decent salary so I can hire somebody to take care of the studio."

"That sounds reasonable," Pete replied. "I'm prepared to offer 10% of the business and a handsome salary."

That quickly, Craze got drawn back into the band business.

After remodeling the interior of the bar, Craze pulled out all the stops and attacked the job at hand. He used all his past connections and booked acts from all over the country. Located on the second floor of the club, and overlooking the entire first floor,

Pete provided Craze with the coolest office in town; the perfect place to conduct business and entertain VIPs. Besides a desk, the music-memorabilia-filled office also contained an antique couch and stuffed chairs. Pete had also installed a one-way mirror overlooking the first floor so that Craze and his guests could observe the festivities from the comfort of his office. In later years, Craze thought, "I had my own 'sky box' before 'sky boxes' were invented."

Finally, to top everything off, Pete supplied AN OLD PINBALL MACHINE. Besides providing outstanding entertainment, Craze made radical changes to "how bars were run" at the time. One of the major changes included getting rid of all the huge male bouncers and doormen and replacing them with women. He thought, "Who's stupid enough to fight with a girl? Belligerent drunks won't have an excuse to fight with big tough bouncers; I think they're more likely to listen to a girl."

Of course, when trouble occurred, Craze handled the problem himself...of course backed by the mild mannered "Gruesome Drew-some," a six-foot-nine Frankenstein look-alike. In the rare event that trouble started, Craze would say to the offender something like, "Hey, knock it off or get out of here!"

With their manhood challenged by Craze's words, the violator always responded with, "So, you think you're big enough to stop me?"

Craze would simply answer, "NO, BUT HE IS!" pointing to an evil-smiling Gruesome Drew-some who always stood right behind Craze when trouble started. That tactic immediately solved the dispute.

To make the system work, Craze taught all the employees a special hand-signal that meant, "Craze come immediately to my location."

One night, Craze got the hand-signal from the "door girl." As he made his way to the main door, Craze politely worked his way through the crowd saying, "Excuse me, excuse me." On the other hand, Gruesome Drew-some made his way to the door like Frankenstein, unintentionally plowing through customers and knocking them over like bowling pins in a bowling alley.

"Were we robbed? Is there a fight?" Craze thought, as he got to the door. "Everything looks pretty peaceful."

With adrenaline still flowing, Craze asked the door girl, "What's the problem?"

She pointed to a tall skinny guy with dark curly hair and answered, "This guy said you told him that he could get in for free and get free drinks all night."

Now angry, and still full of adrenaline, Craze angrily stared at the guy and thought, "I never seen this guy, is he trying to pull a fast one; who is he?"

The door girl shouted over the loud music, "He says his name is Tom Shipley of *Brewer and Shipley*."

Craze immediately changed his attitude, put his arm around Shipley and said, "Welcome Tom, come on in. Drinks are on the house; let me introduce you to the bartender."

Then thinking to himself: "Just the type of people I want hanging out at the bar and I almost threw him out."

𝄞

With everything in place, Craze began turning *Ford's* into a huge success, and his past connections went to bat for him.

Paul, the manager of *The Ozark Mountain Daredevils,* came to Craze with a great proposal: "Craze, here's my plan. My company has bands traveling across the country that are either first-album bands, or bands being seasoned to become national recording artists. As these bands travel between big cities like St. Louis, Kansas City, Denver, and Chicago, they're just killing time between engagements. During these down-times, they also need to eat and sleep, and that situation costs money.

CHAPTER 11

"I propose using *Fords* as a laboratory, so to speak, which would allow our bands an extra place to show their wares. We can kill two birds with one stone. They can stay overnight in Columbia, play for the *Ford's* crowd, and in return, earn hotel rooms and food, getting rid of costly overhead. Your cost: rooms, food, and beverages; your benefit, guaranteed high-quality entertainment on week nights."

Craze sealed the deal. He now had access to high-quality bands at a bargain price. In return, the bands picked up a paid stopover and a quality place to show their wares. Craze immediately worked a deal with the hotel next door. Craze provided comfortable rooms only steps away from the club and free food and drink during their stay. Ironically, Tookie's new "southern rock" band became the biggest draw and most profitable band to play at *Ford's Theater*.

Craze brought *Ford's* all the way back from a broken-down old DJ bar to the most popular place in the area. *Ford's Theater* became known for their quality entertainment and consistently packed houses. If you came to *Ford's*, you were guaranteed seeing an excellent band even if you had never heard of them before.

Craze had become extremely busy at *Ford's*, so he hired a manager for *The Glassworks*. After managing the business for a lengthy period of time, the manager came to him with an offer that Craze couldn't refuse. The guy pointed outside the studio window and said, "Craze look at that empty store front across the street. I'm going to make you an offer for your part of this business, and you're going to accept my offer. If you don't, I'm moving into that location down there and will put you out of business. I know for a fact that you're too busy with *Ford's*, so I think you should take my deal."

Craze thought, "He's got me by the short hairs. He's done his homework and he knows that I don't have the time to take the shop back." Craze was forced to sell *Village Glassworks*.

𝄞

Two weeks later while he packed his personal belongings, Craze took his last looks out the windows of *Village Glassworks*. As Craze continued packing, Pete, the owner of *Ford's* stopped in.

"Craze I've got news for you. I JUST SOLD *FORD'S THEATER*. The business has reached its peak, and I've been offered a premium price for the bar."

That was it... *Ford's* was sold. Craze went from the busiest and happiest guy on the planet, to unemployed and crushed by music one more time.

"Every time I reach the pinnacle in this business, I get shot down and have to start over again. The same things that make me good at what I do in music seem to lead to my downfalls. I care too much, get lost in the business, and fail to keep an eye on what's going on around me. It's like I help create these monsters, and they end up devouring me. Man, music has brought nothing but heartache and failure. I've had it, and this time I MEAN IT."

Chapter 12

Del Alma

Craze had lived the life of a "civilian" for many years: working, getting married, and raising two kids. One day, Craze's dad asked, "You know, I haven't heard you talk about music for a long time. What's going on?"

Craze answered, "Well dad, it's like this. I got hurt a lot playing music, so I gave it up. I can't even listen to music without bringing up bad feelings."

His dad paused and said, "That's interesting; I had the same thing happen to me. For years after your uncle died, every time I heard forties music, it reminded me of him, and the memories were just too painful. A couple of years ago, I heard *Dean Martin* singing, and since then, for some reason, the music reminds me of all the good times that I had with your uncle, not his death."

A light bulb went off in Craze's head, and he thought, "You know what, I've never thought about all the successes that I had in music; I've only focused on the failures. Really, if I think about it, those years were well-spent and well worth remembering."

From then on, Craze proudly looked back at his time in music… and he could even listen to music again.

Hearing music from a distance always excited Craze, and what he heard this time got his attention. The deep rumble of the bass guitar and drums combined with the floating high notes of the keyboard and guitar got his blood flowing. He picked up his step as he got closer to the source of this far-off music, a free outside concert in downtown Columbia. He had never heard anything like this wonderfully strange music. He thought, "It's like "Mexican jazz" or something…and listen to that guitar! That guy can play! I guess the city put up money and hired a national act."

He entered the open-air amphitheater and joined the large crowd. As usual, he worked his way to the back row of the seating, built into the naturally sloped hill facing the stage. To him, the back row was always the best seat in the house. From this vantage point, he could observe both the band and the audience's reactions. Settled in, he focused his attention on the stage. What he heard from the mixed nationality, eight-piece band named *Del Alma* put his brain on tilt.

"I've been around a long time and I've never heard anything like this kind of music. It definitely has a Mexican flavor to it, but so much more sophisticated. Man, they are good! This music is almost sexual."

Craze focused his attention on the tall slender, dark-straight-haired "white" guitar player passionately attacking his guitar. Craze thought, "He sounds like he's playing six guitars at once. He's so fast and smooth; he's definitely not human. He's as good as anybody that I've ever heard in the business. I feel like I'm witnessing history in the making again…and this guitar player almost looks as good on stage as the music he's playing."

The crowd's response to each song told Craze that they completely agreed with his opinion. Then, he noticed a couple of local guys playing in the band. He thought, "Maybe these guys left town and hit the big time. I don't know anybody around this

part of the woods that could put something like this together."...
Or so he thought.

Things had obviously changed while Craze had exiled himself from music. After the concert, Craze approached the bass player, Pete, an old friend and local musician. Craze always felt a sense of pride being associated with great people like Pete, a down-to-earth, friendly and honest guy...AND great musician.

Craze asked, "Hey Pete, what happened; did you hit the big time and join a national act? This band is great. Where are they from?"

Pete replied, "No man, I wish... we're local. This guy Alfredo came to town from El Salvador a few years ago and introduced us to this Latino thing. He formed this band and we've been playing together ever since. He's a stickler for perfection, but that's a good thing."

Craze responded, "Man, you aren't kidding; it really shows in the performance. I am really impressed. You guys got any irons in the fire nationally?"

"I don't think so, but you'll have to ask Alfredo, he's in charge of everything."

"One more question, Pete... who's that guitar player?"

"Oh, he's local; good, isn't he? Let me introduce you to Alfredo."

Pete took Craze over to the medium height, well-built, black-wavy-haired, dark-skinned Alfredo. The tough-faced Latino spoke with an easily understood Spanish accent, "I'm so glad to meet you Craze; what can I do for you?"

"It's an honor to meet you too, Alfredo. First of all, allow me to compliment you and your band; your music is outstanding. Do you mind if I ask you if you have any leads with recording companies or national booking agents?"

Alfredo guardedly answered, "I might have some things in mind. Why do you ask?"

"Well, I have some contacts that might be able to help. Would you mind meeting some time after I make some inquiries? By the way, do you have any recordings just in case we might need them?"

"Yes we do."

Next, Pete introduced Craze to Will, the guitar player. Craze said, "Will, you are one of the best pickers I've ever heard and it's an honor to make your acquaintance."

Will bashfully answered, "Dude, thanks."

Craze thought, "It's amazing how some of these young phenoms are so shy when you talk to them but turn into tigers when they get on stage in front of a crowd."

As he left the amphitheater, Craze thought, "EYES HAS GOT TO HEAR THESE GUYS."

After discussing *Del Alma* with Eyes, he said, "Sure Craze, I'd be glad to listen to anything you have. If they're as good as you say they are, I'll pass them on the appropriate record labels.

"Thanks man, I appreciate your help."

With that information under his belt, Craze contacted Alfredo and passed on the information.

During the next several weeks, Alfredo and Craze took time to get to know each other. Alfredo originally came from El Salvador and moved to the U.S. to avoid the unrest in his country. Classically trained on the French horn, he had previously performed with orchestras on the East Coast, eventually ending up in Columbia, playing for the *Missouri Symphony*. At that point, he formed *Del Alma*.

Craze soon learned two things about Alfredo. First of all, he WAS *Del Alma,* heart and soul, and nobody questioned his authority. He ran this band, no question. Second of all, Alfredo had been around the block and protected his creation by being skeptical of any propositions that came their way.

That information suited Craze just fine, totally agreeing with both positions. Craze thought, "Bands work better in 'dictatorships' than 'democracies' anyway. Most of time 'democracies' water down the final product. And being skeptical from past bad experiences is right up my alley."

Alfredo taught Craze about the Latino culture. Names like Salsa, Meringue, and Cumbia defined the different styles of Latino music. In forming *Del Alma*, Alfredo had melded the different groups of music together, which must have offended some Latinos.

Alfredo described a caste-like system among Latinos based on where they came from and the darkness of their skin: "Craze, you must understand that in the Latino culture, the lighter your skin, the higher one ranks in the society. Most importantly, where you were born is of tremendous importance. The European Spanish and Cubans rank the highest, followed by the South Americans and Caribbean people. Finally Central Americans and Mexicans occupy the bottom. As far as *Del Alma* is concerned, we get much better reactions from mixed crowds, both white and Latino, than we do from strictly Latino audiences."

A trip to Chicago demonstrated these facts. Alfredo explained, "We played two engagements; one club consisted of a mixed crowd and the other club had mostly Cubans. At the mixed crowd engagement, they danced on the bar and had a great time. The other, Cuban, engagement produced a completely different reaction. My dark skin gave away my heritage. When they found out that I came from El Salvador, things got much worse. First of all, they charged the band for parking the van that we hauled our equipment in. Next, they stuck our wives at a table in a separate room where they couldn't see the bandstand. The crowd reacted mildly, at best, to our performance. We played the gig and got out of there."

Eventually, a trust blossomed between Alfredo and Craze and they discussed the possibility of Craze becoming their manager.

Right up front, Craze explained his intentions to Alfredo, "I don't want your money, Alfredo. I have a higher purpose in mind… it's personal; I have something to prove to myself. If we strike a deal with Eyes, then I'll expect my 'just desserts' from the profits of any records; and if I become a full-fledged manager, I'll need money to support my family."

After discussing the details, Craze became the manager. Unexpectedly back in the saddle of music again, Craze attended shows, observing and helping out wherever possible. Feeling comfortable with his relationship with Alfredo, Craze sent the *Del Alma* CD to the now vice president of his record company, Eyes.

"Even though we have sent our CD to Eyes, I think I want to make a second CD. Our sound has evolved and I want a back-up plan if things don't work out."

Alfredo knew the business, and—even with Craze presenting the original CD to Eyes—he understood the odds involved. By producing a new CD, he could keep the band moving forward. Most of all, Alfredo would have peace of mind, a good compromise for his nerves. Alfredo asked, "Craze, do you have any studios in mind? I'm looking for a studio that is willing to push the limits and allow me to create a much brighter sound than our original CD."

Craze replied, "Let me check some things out, I just might have the perfect person and studio in mind."

Craze's first thought flashed back to his old partner in crime, Lawder, who owned a small recording studio in St. Louis. After discussing Alfredo's requirements, Lawder realized that his studio could not handle such a large project. But he had another studio in mind. With excitement in his voice, Lawder said, "You know what Craze? I might have the perfect place to do this project… and the perfect engineer to produce it. Let me check some things out and get back to you."

So Lawder put together the perfect studio and the perfect team, filling all of Alfredo's wishes. The team included and an old musician friend from back in the day, named Dave, to engineer the project. His laid-back personality allowed Alfredo all the room he needed to push the limits of his crisp sound ideas. Lawder also joined the project as a co-producer with Alfredo. Craze, as usual, became the glue holding the project together and solving any disputes.

Putting his project in the hands of strangers made Alfredo a little leery, but by now he trusted Craze's judgment. This trust demonstrated a great leap of faith for Alfredo. This new trust convinced Craze that Alfredo had turned a corner in their relationship.

To Craze's shock, Will, the fabulous lead guitar player, caused the only real problems. Will's dilemma blindsided the group. The most accomplished musician in the room choked in the studio. Over and over, he could not get his parts down, causing cost overruns in the budget. Craze thought, "Man, it goes to show you, just because somebody's outstanding at one thing, doesn't mean he can shine at everything."

After polishing up the final product, the CD was completed.

Alfredo asked, "Craze, I have a problem and I hope you might be able to help me. We have an important gig at a bar in St. Louis and our keyboard player can't make it. Do you have anyone in mind who might be able to fill in?"

Craze knew one person who was capable of playing ANYTHING on the keyboards, including Latino music. Without hesitation, Craze answered, "Yeah, I know a guy, let me do some checking. He's a busy man, so I'll have to see if he's available."

"If anybody can handle this situation, PETER can," Craze thought. "But I'm not sure if he has the time or if he'll be up for doing a non-classical project."

Craze spoke to Peter, "Hey man, I've got a huge favor to ask. Would you play a bar gig in St. Louis with *Del Alma*? You're the only one I know that's capable of filling in on such short notice."

After hesitating, Peter answered, "Well, I guess so if there's nobody else. How am I gonna learn this music? Since you guys are in Columbia and I'm in St. Louis, how will we rehearse? How will I learn the songs?"

Craze answered, "I've got that problem solved. We have two CDs that accurately represent their songs. Lawder co-produced one of them. I'll send you copies and you can learn your parts from them."

"Since it's you, I'll do it," Peter answered.

Craze thought, "That completes the circle. I never thought that I'd see the day that Eyes, Lawder, Peter, and I would come together one more time on a musical project. Wonders never cease."

After playing the gig, Peter told Craze, "Craze, I was worried when you asked me to do the gig. It took everything in me to say yes. I never thought that I'd ever enter a drinking establishment. But you needed help, so I did it. And I have to admit, even though people were drinking, which bothered me, I forgot how good musicians who played in bars could be. The guys in *Del Alma* restored my faith in quality musicianship in that field of endeavor...they're outstanding musicians. But remember this, you're the only person in the world that I would have done this for."

Humbled, Craze answered, "Thank you, again."

𝄞

And then there was: "Craze this CD has some very interesting stuff. *Del Alma* has a very unique sound. So, if it's okay with you, I'll pass the CD on to our VP of the 'World Beat' division. I believe that this category best fits *Del Alma's* genre. Now understand this clearly. The CD has to stand on its own. I will not influence any label in my company to take on this project, but I think it's unique enough to stir some interest…no promises you understand."

Craze replied, "Thanks man, this means a lot to me. I owe you a big one."

Thanks to his always-loyal old friend Eyes, Craze had just accomplished getting *Del Alma* in the front door of one of the largest record conglomerates in the world. Going over possible scenarios that might come up, the two old buddies talked for an hour and a half. Eyes recommended things like protecting each other's interests with a legal agreement between Alfredo and Craze. Eyes said, "Iron out a deal and get it in writing; you'll both feel more comfortable moving on. Then, when questions arise, there won't be any surprises."

"Craze, there's no difference between what you're doing now and what you did taking care of the 'business end' in *The Public Service*. This job fits you like a glove, so run with it, you'll do just fine."

Craze thought, "Well I did it. I successfully presented a band to a record company and got them in the front door. Whatever happens from here on out, at least I know my musical instincts are still in tact. Because of Eyes, we're gonna be heard by the best in the business and that's all anybody could ask."

Craze called Alfredo and gave him the good news, "Congratulations brother, the record company called and they're interested. The best in the business are hearing your music as we speak."

Neither Craze nor Alfredo had ever been this close to signing with a big label, and they shared their excitement. For the first time, Craze felt real excitement in Alfredo's voice: "Thank you Craze, I guess we now find out if we have what it takes."

"Hi, my name is Robert and I work at Eyes's record company. I walked by the 'World Beat' office the other day and I heard this music coming from the office. The music was your *Del Alma* CD. I made some inquiries and was told to contact you about using your music in a movie project that I'm working on. The movie is called *The Love Police*. The movie is about the adventures of an L.A. mafia guy and his girlfriend. Their quest takes them from L.A. to Miami. The filming of the movie will take place in those two locations. Your music is exactly what I'm looking for. I would like to know if you might be interested in allowing me to use your music in my movie."

Craze contacted Eyes to make sure that this guy was legit. Eyes answered, "Yeah, he's legit, but just remember, eighty percent of these movie projects never see the light of day for one reason or the other; mostly money. So don't get your hopes up. I do think it's worth pursuing if for no other reason than to get the experience, and it might be fun going through the process."

So after coming to an agreement with Robert, Alfredo and Craze began their adventure in movie making.

Craze appreciated the openness of Robert. He made sure that Alfredo and Craze were constantly updated every step of the way. First of all, he left the record company, totally devoting his time to the project. Next he sent a copy of the script for the guys to read.

Robert explained, "As you already know, the setting for the movie takes place in L.A. and Miami. I've completed all the details here in L.A., like film locations, crews, and investors, and I have the money secured for this part of the movie. I'm headed to Miami to finalize the details there."

Craze thought, "Well, Eyes said that most of these movie projects fail. But so far so good with this one."

CHAPTER 12

Robert kept Craze apprised of his latest encounters as he traveled across the country looking for more investors. Craze thought, "Eyes was right. Being involved in Robert's quest is exciting."

One day Robert called from Miami and informed Craze that he had found a film crew. Then he explained, "Craze, I've reached 'make it or break it' time. I'm convening with my last and biggest investor. If things go right with this investor, we have a 'green light' to make the movie."

Craze never heard from Robert again. Weeks passed and Robert never called. He vanished into thin air. He never answered his phone or called Craze back.

"I don't know, maybe he died or something," Craze thought. "I guess the investor probably rejected the proposal."

Craze never saw advertising for a movie called *The Love Police*.

𝄞

Paul (*Daredevils* and *Ford's*) called Craze with a proposal. "Craze, I've set up a new production company in L.A., and I've got a project that your band, *Del Alma,* might be interested in. I've hooked up to a project with an old friend from my days at *The University of Missouri*. He's moved to Hawaii and started a guitar manufacturing company. But this guitar is different. It's made from 100% graphite materials, and it's guaranteed to never go out of tune. I'm supervising the promotion of this new guitar. Part of my job includes looking for big-name endorsements. But I'm also looking for 'up and coming' musicians and bands. *Del Alma* immediately came to mind as a band on their way up in the industry."

Craze immediately gave Paul the go-ahead to use *Del Alma* in their promotions. Craze thought, "No brainer, a 'win/win' no matter how you look at it. Free publicity now and free guitars if we get a recording deal."

"Craze I'm planning a trip to Kansas City," Paul said. "If the band wants to try a graphite guitar, I could drive to Columbia and drop one off for a time. Look through the promotional material and pick one out."

Craze readily agreed, and Will picked out the one he fancied, an acoustic guitar with built-in pickups. Craze called Paul with their choice, and they set a date for his visit. In the meantime, Craze came up with the great idea.

"Alfredo, let's not waste this opportunity. Paul's an important connection, so let's set up a gig so Paul can hear the band live."

A winery located on a cliff overlooking the Missouri River east of Columbia offered the perfect site for the event. The winery loved the idea, and so did Paul, so they set the date for an afternoon gig. They met at the winery, and Paul presented Will with the chosen guitar. William took the guitar off to the side and familiarized himself with it, while Paul and Craze found a seat and prepared for the show. As *Del Alma* performed, Paul leaned over to Craze and said, "Hey man, they're even better live than their recordings, and Will is as good as advertised. If your recording deal doesn't work out, I'd love to have a shot at selling them."

After the show, Craze thought, "*Del Alma* did themselves proud today, playing their usual flawless show. And the picturesque background didn't hurt."

As Paul prepared for his trip back to Kansas City, he said, "Why don't you guys keep that guitar for a while; just send it back to me when you're finished."

After a few weeks of Will and Alfredo having fun playing the guitar, Craze sent the guitar back.

𝄞

Week after week, Eyes kept Craze posted on the progress of the CD. Each conversation started with, "I have another label interested in *Del Alma*. They're passing the CD on to their people to see if they can do anything with it."

Each time, the same answer came back: "They loved the CD, but the marketing department cannot figure out how to sell it. The unique sound doesn't fit into any of their markets."

The rejections kept coming in from the different record labels, all with the same response. "They just don't know how to sell this project!"

Eyes finally said, "Craze, I'm running out of ideas. None of my labels are interested. If you want me to, I'll pass the CD on to other labels that I'm not associated with. But I think the response will be the same. Just tell me what you want me to do and I'll be glad to help."

"No man, I don't want to waste any more of your time. You gave it your best shot and that's all anybody could ask. I want you to know how much I appreciate you going out on a limb for me."

"Well thanks Craze, but don't ever think that you're wasting my time. I was glad to help."

Craze thought, "I have one more bullet left in the chamber. Maybe Paul might have some better luck with his contacts."

After several weeks of trying, Paul came back with the same responses, "They don't know how to sell this music."

In all, twenty-nine record labels rejected *Del Alma* with every label responding with the same answer. Alfredo had a theory: "Nobody has ever tried to combine the various types of Latino music like I've done with *Del Alma*. I guess the world is just not ready yet for my style of music."

Although disappointed by the results, Craze felt proud that his friends stepped forward and helped in every way to assist in his latest dream. Completely out of bullets, the time had arrived for Craze to say good-bye to Alfredo and *Del Alma*.

"Alfredo, all I can do now is stand around and look pretty. And 'that' isn't gonna do anybody any good."

As he left Alfredo, Craze thought, "So close, but still so far away."

Deadly influences

Several months after the demise of Del Alma, Will, the fabulous lead guitar player, contacted Craze about a new project. "Hey man," he said. "I started a new rock-a-billy trio and wondered if you might be interested in helping me out."

Immediately excited by the possibility of working with such a tremendous talent, Craze replied, "Sure let's get together and talk about it."

Craze's mind went wild thinking about the possibilities of working with Will's unbelievable guitar playing.

"This guy could possibly become the next Eric Clapton or Jimi Hendrix. But first, he'll have to discover his personal unique style and personality."

Then, Will told Craze about his plan. "Man, I'm gonna write songs and do all the singing. And of course, I'll also play lead guitar."

Craze had lofty goals for Will, but he sensed major snags with Will's plan. "Wait a minute, writing songs, and singing lead…RED FLAG? Why do these guys with so much God-given talent always want to do something else? Just because he's an outstanding guitar player doesn't automatically make great at everything else. Well, with Will's amazing guitar skills, I might as well see where this thing is headed."

So Craze got together with Will's new band. The trio included an ex-Marine and truly nice guy, Blaine, on bass and a fabulous drummer named John. The three guys formed a tight, cohesive unit and, with the proper guidance, this project had great potential. But over time, problems slowly reared their ugly faces.

First of all, Will didn't write very good songs. But he insisted on playing them anyway. Craze tried helping by suggesting original songs written by his friends and researching old obscure songs that the band could modify into their own style. But Will ignored all of Craze's suggestions. Second of all, Will sang okay, but his voice wasn't strong enough to sing leads. Craze suggested finding a lead singer, but that idea also fell on deaf ears.

Craze did find one shining light in the band, but it took a while. For several months, John the outstanding drummer said absolutely nothing to Craze; not one word. He just stared at Craze expressionless while Craze talked. Craze's mind conjured up theories about this strange fellow: "Sitting there, he reminds me of a block of concrete. Maybe he's stupid or thinks I'm lying? He might think I'm going to steal all his money; or worse yet, maybe he's planning on stealing my money? I hope he doesn't show up at my door some day and kill my family. This guy isn't right in the head. I'm gonna keep at least one eyeball on him at all times."

John paid attention to every word Craze said but never made a comment or displayed any feelings. One evening after six months of the silent treatment, Craze felt a touch on his shoulder. Craze turned and there stood John the drummer. Taken by surprise, Craze jumped back. For the first time, John spoke, "Craze, can I speak to you in private for a second?"

Craze thought, "Oh God here we go!"

"Craze, I get it. I get your point. I see where you're going with your ideas about bands and I agree 100%. Count me in."

That whole time, John had been studying Craze, weighing his theories and memorizing everything that came out of his mouth. At that moment, John and Craze became close friends. Later on in life when Craze encountered band management problems, he called on John for help. Best of all, Craze got introduced to John's strange sense of humor.

If circumstances were not bad enough already, things really started unraveling. One night, during a break at a gig, Craze noticed Will sitting at a table, talking to a fairly attractive young lady. It was "love at first sight." True love blossomed, and she immediately took over every aspect of Will's life. Craze thought, "Uh oh, I've seen this movie before. These outside influences can be disastrous, and girlfriends who don't understand the program are the worst."

From then on, she took her position at a table with an unobstructed view of her new man. Craze also noticed that William no longer played to the audience but focused all of his attention on serenading his girl. John dubbed her "Psycho."

Psycho even started dressing Will. John could not wait to see "Will's latest fashions." John patiently prepared himself for Will's entrances, and when Will made his appearance, John would laugh hysterically, usually falling on the floor, saying things like, "Who dressed you this time?" or "Man, those eighties-style shiny pants really make you stand out in a crowd."

John confessed to Craze, "I'm not trying to be mean, but we've been best friends for years, and he keeps falling for these girls who want to change him. I do this to embarrass him into seeing what they're doing to him. It doesn't work. But I'll keep it up. Maybe someday he'll get the hint…but you do have to admit that it is pretty entertaining."

Psycho started showing up at rehearsals. Constantly checking her watch, "Yoko, I mean Psycho" always took her position next to Will. After a couple of minutes, she would whisper something in Will's ear, then using some lame excuse, Will would announce that he had to leave.

The situation reached a breaking point when Will started canceling rehearsals and showing up late for gigs. Red-faced and stressed, Will told Craze, "She wants me to give up music and find a real job."

Will continued playing, but from then on, he went from a cool, fun, happy-go-lucky guy to a complete mess. When asked, Will always stated that music was the most important thing in his life. But in reality, Will's brain went somewhere else, and rehearsals and progress ceased. Craze thought, "I don't understand these girls. They fall in love with these guys in bands, and then they get jealous of the attention and try to destroy the very reason that they were interested in the guy in the first place. Man, these outside influences can kill a band...especially girlfriends."

Unfortunately, Craze had already sent the sub-par CDs to Eyes. Craze even talked Eyes and Lawder into attending a gig. Already knowing the answer, Craze asked Eyes what he thought. Eyes responded with, "Good bar band."

Craze took the phrase as code for, "you're not good enough," or "the kiss of death" in the recording industry, which Will's band certainly deserved.

Another example of deadly outside influences

Hilary, her husband, Michael, and Craze sat around the coffee table having their latest band meeting. The beautiful young blond woman and her handsome, wild dark-haired husband played in a band featuring her many original songs. Hilary painted exquisite pictures of past failed loves with her heart-breaking songs. Classically trained, she sometimes played an electric piano and sometimes played a fiddle to get her point across. But her "perfect pitch" voice made the whole thing worthwhile.

Craze thought as he observed the two sitting across from him: "You couldn't come up with a better picture than these two on stage...the young innocent 'damsel in distress' singing and playing violin, center stage, while her 'alter ego,' uninhibited cave man-like husband circled her with his African djembe drum hanging around his neck in pursuit of her affections. I don't know why, but Michael reminds me of Tarzan pursuing Jane."

Tonight's task: have the couple critique the *Judy Collins* concert that they had recently attended. Craze had worked with the band for quite some time and hoped that they might bring home some pearls of wisdom from one of the best in the business. He wanted to use the *Judy Collins* concert as a learning experience for their upcoming *Fourth of July* show at the football stadium playing in front of thousands of people attending the fireworks display. Ironically, *Del Alma* was on the same bill.

After some small talk, Hilary said, "I did like you asked and paid close attention to Judy's concert; and you know what Craze? Judy does a strange thing. After every song, she pushes the mic away from her face, and then when she gets ready to speak again she moves it back to exactly the same spot. After a while, it became real noticeable, almost irritating."

Craze seized the moment and said, "That's interesting. Do you realize that you have your own little quirks on stage?"

Baffled, she replied, "No, what's that?"

"Well you apologize a lot; in fact, you apologize a WHOLE lot. You constantly say things like, 'Sorry I'm out of tune. Sorry I have to change instruments. Sorry my voice is scratchy tonight...sorry I'm responsible for every problem in the world.' Do you get my point? Never draw attention to mistakes. Most audiences don't hear the mistakes, so you're needlessly making them aware of the negative aspects of your performance. It leaves a bad impression of YOU in their minds."

Hilary never apologized again on stage.

The band showed up for their sound check the afternoon of the show, and Craze immediately recognized the sound guy. He thought, "Well, there's a break; they hired one of the best sound guys in the area."

CHAPTER 12

So during the sound check, Craze made himself at home in the sound booth. He asked, "Hey man, you mind if I make suggestions during the show? I know what needs to happen and when with this band."

"Of course not. I can use all the help I can get!"

Craze thought, "Man you can tell the best sound guys in the business. They don't feel threatened by others and welcome any help they can get."

That evening, as Alfredo and *Del Alma* finished their set, Hilary and company gathered out of sight. Under the stands before their show, Craze noticed a guy in golf cart.

"Hey man, can I ask you for a big favor?"

"Sure what?"

"When our band is announced, will you drive Hilary to the front of the stage and drop her off?" Catching Craze's plan, he said, "Not at all man, I like the way you think."

Craze huddled the band around him as he explained his last-minute plan.

"Everybody, go out there and get ready. Bill (the guitar player), get Hilary's equipment ready for her. When everybody is ready, start playing. Bill, make a big deal introduction while she enters the stadium. Let's make her look like a star."

Right on cue, Bill made his announcement, and Craze sent Hilary off from under the stands. Hilary entered the stadium waving to the huge crowd while they cheered her on. On stage, Hilary had never looked better. Taking control of the show, she gave the performance of her life. Now positioned in the sound booth, Craze joined the soundman, sat back, and enjoyed the show. Hilary captured the audience with her charm and music, while Michael circled around her with his djembe drum looking like "The Wild Man of Borneo."

After the finale and a great reception from the audience, Craze joined Hilary on stage. As she packed her equipment, Craze gave her a well-deserved hug and congratulated her on her excellent performance. He grabbed her hand and said, "Put your equipment down. You're not done yet, follow me."

Hilary gave Craze a confused look as she followed his orders. Craze had noticed the many admiring fans gathering in the front rows behind a four-foot wall that separated the stands from the field. As he guided her to her destination, Craze handed her a pen and said, "Go meet your fans. They're dying to meet you."

The enthusiastic fans gathered around Hilary. While she signed autographs, she talked with them, answering any and all of their questions. Craze stood back and thought, "What a perfect ending to a great performance!"

In the beginning, Craze understood the relationship that Hilary had with her mother. Her mother took on the role as Hilary's manager and personally overlooked all business deals. So Craze understood HIS position. He would shop her music, and any deal that he personally got on his own would be HIS deal. Before going out on a limb, he presented his contract to Hilary and Michael. Hilary's mother had also read the contract. Nothing had to be signed right now, but when the rubber hit the road, these were his terms.

After the Fourth of July gig, the time had come for Eyes to hear the music, so Craze sent the CD off and waited for his response. In the meantime, Craze needed a signed contract to protect his interests in this deal. Up to this point, Craze had not taken a penny for his months-long efforts, nor did he expect any. But from here on out, he needed assurances. The details of the contract had been discussed between Hilary, Michael, and Craze many months earlier, so Craze considered this effort a mere formality, and now, the couple needed to sign the contract.

CHAPTER 12

As he entered the room, Hilary held back tears. Craze thought, "Not a very good start. Her mother obviously got to her. I bet her mother thinks I'm some sort of shyster."

"My mom and I want to know why you think you're worth such a large percentage of the business. You're asking for 12½ percent of my lifelong works. What makes you think you're worth that much?"

Not completely surprised by the question, Craze calmly said, "I understand your concern. But look at this from my standpoint. First of all, up to this point, I've provided my services free of charge, and that's fine. You've been in the business for what, ten years, maybe twenty? Well, it's taken me forty years to gain the trust and make the connections so that I CAN offer you this opportunity.

"But, please answer this question: Why are you questioning this now? This is not a surprise. You've had a copy of this contract for months and you've known all along what I expected. As a matter of fact, if you and your mother checked things out on your end, this contract is 2½ percent less than the suggested standard rate. What did you think was going to happen at this point? You've never said a word about having second thoughts."

Craze thought, "A classic case of getting cold feet. They want their cake and eat it too…Well it ain't gonna work! Why didn't I see this coming? I should have paid more attention to her mom getting in the way."

"I was afraid that if I told you, you would leave, and the whole deal would fall through. I didn't want to lose the chance of getting a contract through your people."

Craze thought, "Stalemate, time to leave!"

Craze noticed during the whole conversation, Michael did not say a word. Craze continued, "Well, I guess there's nothing more to discuss. So I'll be on my way. If you have a change of heart, give me a call, but don't wait too long. These things have a way of slipping away."

As he left, Craze knew that if Eyes ever caught wind of this conversation, he would immediately trash the project. Craze thought, "The last thing Eyes needs is trouble."

𝄞

Not long after the incident, Eyes and Craze talked about everything under the sun...EXCEPT Hilary. Finally Eyes said, "Oh, by the way, I asked around, and I can't do anything with that girl you're working with."

Craze thought, "Uh-oh, it's time to quit bothering Eyes."

They finished their conversation with their friendship still intact. Craze realized his mistake and finally hung up his musical career permanently.

𝄞

But this time he left the music business with a completely different attitude.

"This business can kill you, but I made it; I survived and flourished. What a ride! I wouldn't give up my experiences for anything in the world. The people I've met along the way made my life worth living. I've managed to make it completely around the block in the music business, experiencing it from every angle. I've played an instrument, managed bands, run clubs and functioned as a talent agent.

"We played with some of the best bands in the world and got to hang out with them. Just think, we actually played with *Canned Heat, Steppenwolf, Jefferson Airplane, Quicksilver Messenger Service*...and *The Grateful Dead*, among others. And let's not forget our heroes, *Duane and Greg Allman*. They showed us the light; best of all, the great *Albert King* offered me a job, and let's not forget *Chuck Berry*. They all helped make my dreams possible."

Chapter 13

End of the Rainbow

Throughout the days in the band, the guys assigned Craze the position of "Leader of the Band" and basically the "Chief Cook and Bottle Washer" of all things. Those titles, among others things, meant that Craze booked most of the jobs, took care of the money, and kept track of all updates and communications between the guys. But mostly the title meant that any time one of the guys didn't feel like doing a task, they could dump the dirty work on Craze by simply announcing, "Well, we took a vote and you won," OR, "Well, you're the leader, so it's your job."

After the band broke up, the guys made sure that Craze KEPT those designations. When given a task, Craze always acted upset, but in actuality, he felt honored that the guys trusted him; and the titles also gave him an excuse to stay in contact with each one of them. So Craze kept notes, lots of notes, and threw them in the "notes drawer" in his desk.

𝄞

Craze sat down at his desk and prepared himself for the task at hand. Since the drawer had never been cleaned out, he looked down at a completely stuffed drawer overflowing with hunks of paper hanging out the top. Out of fear of forgetting things, Craze took notes—lots of notes—when one of the guys called or communicated with him. When the urge hit him, he "took a note" then filed it in one of two places. The notes that needed immediate attention moved to the side of the top of his desk where they were later transferred to the master list of "things to do." The rest of the notes got shoved into the drawer where he planned to look at them later. But "later" never happened. So after years of filling the drawer, the drawer could no longer handle one more piece of scrap paper.

WHAT Craze took notes ON created a real problem. He tried keeping a note-pad on his desk, but he quickly used up the pads and ended up writing on anything he could get his hands on, like the backs of used envelopes and torn pieces of paper. While driving, a napkin or the back of a receipt served his purpose. So the drawer finally filled up with small chunks of paper containing the valuable information.

Craze boldly opened the drawer and thought about *Spanky's (The Little Rascals)* favorite line, "Well, here goes nothin'." He removed the first hunk of paper and tried to read what had been written on it.

Reading out loud, Craze said, "'Most of the gases in Christmas cao sodtion'... What??? Let me try again, 'Most of this goes in the Christmas card section'...got it."

Note after note presented the same problem: Craze couldn't read his own horrible handwriting! A thought popped into his head: "Now I know what Eyes went through when I handed him his set-list and he'd say, 'do you really expect me to read these 'chicken scratchins?' Wait a minute, I must have a note in here somewhere with that quote on it; maybe I better make another one so I don't forget."

Craze plowed through the endless pile of notes placing each one in its proper place.

"This one goes in Lawder's pile, here's one about Peter"... and so on and so on.

Before long, the top of Craze's desk overflowed with hunks of barely-legible hunks of paper. Frustrated by his dilemma, Craze looked for a solution.

"I'll just dump the whole drawer on the floor. There's plenty of room down there." So Craze pulled out the drawer and dumped the contents in the middle of the floor. He immediately recognized that every note now lay facedown on the floor. Craze thought, "Damn, too late now."

Craze soon realized that by turning the drawer upside down, he had unwittingly put the notes in chronological order. The notes now became a history of Craze's life with the guys. As he turned over each chunk of paper and deciphered the quickly written "chicken scratchins," wonderful memories filled his mind.

FIRST, EYES'S FILE
"Dead Equipment"

Craze's mind flashed back to a couple of days before *The Grateful Dead* concert when Eyes and Craze hung out at the *Velvet Plastic* office, and Jorge needed somebody to drive a truck to the airport to pick up the *Dead's* equipment. Smelling a few extra bucks, in unison, Eyes and Craze asked, "How much?" After settling on a price, the two came up with a plan to overcome a few minor details, like Craze having a broken wrist and Eyes not seeing well enough to drive the large truck. Actually, neither had ever driven a large truck before. Craze thought, "He drives a bike and his car, but I'm not sure how he ever got a driver's license. Oh well, we'll come up with something…I hope."

As they hatched their scheme, Eyes spoke up first, "Hey man, trust me. We got this. It's gonna be 'a piece of cake.' Between the two of us, we make one good driver; so here's what we're gonna do. You can't steer or work the pedals, so I'll do that. Craze, all you need to do is point me in the right direction and tell me which way to go. You'll be the eyes and do the shifting; I'll do the rest."

Craze thought, "Brilliant! Man, I could always count on Eyes to be the brains of the bunch and come up come up with a great plan; this is one of his best."

They crammed themselves into the cab of the truck and sat next to each other in the seat, "boyfriend/girlfriend style" so that Craze could shift. Most importantly, the seating arrangement allowed Craze to provide a second set of eyes to help guide Eyes down the road. Well, it made sense to Craze at the time. So together, they proceeded to the airport.

Craze directed Eyes, "Okay man, get ready; turn here…no, not there, that's a parking place. Go a little farther. Okay, good. Now, see that stop sign…? Well, nobody was coming anyway. We'll just stop a little longer at the next one, and that'll make up for the last one. Eyes, you're doing great. Just slow down a little bit and try not to hit the curb so much."

They pulled up to the airport dock, which meant backing up. Craze thought,

"I forgot about backing up. With all these other trucks in the way, this might be a little tricky."

After a couple of tries, they inched the truck into the dock. Two long-haired biker types walked over to Eyes and Craze and asked, "You dudes from *Velvet Plastic*? We're with *The Dead*."

Craze thought, "After that trip, we almost joined you; 'with the dead,' I mean."

"You Can't Dig Anybody Until You Dig Yourself"

As he had done many times in the past, Craze patiently waited while Eyes carefully chose his words. Craze and the other guys always welcomed the advice from their friend. Wise beyond his years, his opinions mattered. So after Eyes mulled over Craze's desire to get out of town and make a major change in his life, Craze got ready to listen and not interrupt his friend's advice.

Eyes told Craze, "A wise old sage once taught me a great lesson in life. He told me. 'You can't dig anybody until you dig yourself.' Since I heard those words, I've made it my credo in life; and you lived by those words too. But something's changed in your life. You know the sage who said those words to me? YOU DID Craze, and I can tell you this much, you're not digging yourself right now. I don't completely understand why, but that doesn't matter. I do know this for a fact: Something needs to change, and if that means getting out of here, I'm all for it. I'll miss having you around, but that doesn't matter. Don't let the door hit you in the ass. Go find yourself, because I want the old Craze back."

Hearing those words from his best friend, Craze's future suddenly became clear to him. Yes, the time had arrived for him to leave. Craze escaped his hometown to redefine part of his old reality and define part of a new one. This memory from "the drawer" had, of course, preceded the move to Columbia.

"Eyes Majors in Cowboy"

Eyes had just returned from his counselor's visit after his first year of college. As usual, Eyes and Craze sat on the floor of Eyes's room since both thought cushions were cooler than using chairs at the time.

Discussing the events of the interview, Eyes spoke up, "So, today, I'm in my counselor's office, sitting in a chair across the desk from her, and she says, 'Well Mister Eyes, we expect our students to declare a major after their first year of college. Since you've arrived at that plateau, what major do you see in your future?'

"I thought, 'Hell, I don't even want to be here in the first place, but I promised my dad that I wouldn't mess around after high school but go straight to college. He's worried that I if didn't go right away, I'd never go. I also want to major in art, but he'd have a conniption fit. He said he'd financially support me if I used the money to get a 'serious education' and 'art' don't count. This situation left me in a pickle. So I thought for a few seconds and told her, 'Well, why don't you put COWBOY; yeah that's it—cowboy; that's a 'serious education,' isn't it?"

Focusing his attention back to Craze, and not expecting an answer in return, Eyes said, "Craze what difference does it make, WHAT I DECLARE? I'd rather take off on the bike and travel the country. That would give me time to think about my future AND a major. Because of my eyesight, I don't have to worry about the draft like you do. Right now is the perfect time to travel, but it ain't gonna happen. My dad's got me locked-in. Both you and I have had this college education thing drilled into our heads since day one. I know what's gonna end up happening: after I graduate, I'll feel compelled to start a career, leaving no room for the road trip."

So at the counselor's office, his answer remained, "Write down *cowboy* or *neurosurgeon* or *basket weaving*. Hell, I have no idea. I want to use this time studying art, but that's impossible, so those answers make as much sense as anything else."

The counselor said, "Well we'll just leave that space blank for now."

"Eyes Gets Out"

A short while after the band break-up, and as he sunk his teeth more and more into his studies, performing took a back seat to Eyes's education. Later Eyes said to Craze, "Don't get me wrong, I love being on stage, but without the rest of you guys, it just isn't much fun. These other guys I'm playing with are okay, but my heart just isn't in it any more. I feel like I need to move on."

Recalling Eyes's earlier advice about leaving town, Craze responded, "You remember what you told me about 'digging myself'? Well, it sounds like you're not digging yourself right now. It's okay to make a change; it worked out well for me. If performing doesn't fit anymore, get out. Personally I hate to see you leave something you're so good at, but if it's time, it's time."

Eyes replied, "Yeah Craze you're right. I just feel my mind being drawn to a different calling. You know how much I love records. That business has always fascinated me, I guess I'll see where that leads me."

"Eyes has Small Eyeballs Now"

Craze anxiously answered the door of his parents' house expecting to see Eyes on the other side. Both Eyes and Craze found themselves visiting their hometown at the same time, a rare occurrence. They had stayed in contact by phone, but with their busy lives, they hadn't seen each other eye-to-eye in many years. With Eyes living in L.A., and Craze living in Columbia, Missouri, being two thousand miles apart had taken its toll on their old, almost daily face-to-face meetings. Craze opened the door but did not recognize the totally grey shorthaired guy without glasses until the guy spoke. For a second, Craze thought, "Who is this guy?"

Then, the so-familiar voice spoke, "Hey Craze that extra weight looks good on you." Taken by surprise by the words, Craze laughed and immediately recognized Eyes's face and his always-present sly humor. The younger, dashing, dark-haired, tall Eyes with thick glasses had been replaced by an older, no-glasses, and much-greyer shorthaired version of himself. Facing his old friend at the door, Craze jokingly responded, "What happened to the glasses? Your eyeballs look so much smaller without those magnifying glasses on your head. And by the way, why'd you dye your hair that color?"

Eyes fired back, "Yeah, they finally invented contacts that weren't the size of coke-bottle bottoms. You'd think these contacts would be so thick that they'd fall out and sound like plates breaking when they hit the floor. But actually they're amazingly thin...and the hair? Personally I like the color I chose. What do you think?"

"Yeah, well come on in and we'll talk about it."

Welcomed by hugs from Craze's mom and a hearty handshake from his dad, Eyes entered the familiar old living room. Over the years, Eyes's ability to charm people had not changed. Eyes still entered the room and immediately took over. As he had witnessed a thousand times before, Craze smiled as he watched his old friend "work the room" on his family.

Eyes left the record store after accepting a job as a rack jobber in the record business.

Several promotions led him to an eventual move to Los Angeles, and taking care of the big U.S. sales customers. After a little iced tea and conversation with Craze's parents, the two relocated to Craze's comfortable old bedroom in the attic. Eyes leaned back and prepared to speak.

"Man, all this plane travel is a drag. I hate it, but what can I do? It's not the bike trip I had in mind, but it's a gig, and it pays well. Every time I move up to a higher position, it seems like I have to travel more, so I do it because that's what's required."

I just took a new position called Division of Country Sales and Marketing, based in Nashville. It's a flowery name that doesn't describe the real job. I do the dirty work of dealing with 'problem artists,' settling the disputes of disgruntled clients and getting them back on track!"

Craze replied jokingly, "Boy that sounds like lots of fun. It makes me feel glad that I stayed in Columbia."

"I'm not complaining about my success, and I am thankful for the opportunities; but I often do wonder if the whole thing was really worth giving up the things that really mattered the most to me in life."

Tired of talking about himself and getting antsy, Eyes suggested, "Hey man, let's go see your brother's new bar."

"Eyes Will Never Become President"

During a regime change at the record company, Eyes accepted the position of Vice President. His charismatic personality, hard work, good luck, and good fortune finally allowed Eyes to reach an elite status in the industry. He had paid his dues and "made it" to the top of his profession.

Craze naively asked, "Why didn't you ever become president?"

"Are you nuts? Every time there's a change, the president always ends up getting fired first. Being VP guarantees me a job. The new bosses always keep the VP around to show them the ropes and clean up the mess left by the transition."

"Eyes Once Mentioned"

"Hey man, I don't want to get all mushy about this religion thing, but, of all people, I know you'll understand what I'm going through. You and your family were always at church, and I didn't have that experience in my family. So for the first time in my life, I'm getting involved in a spiritual life. It feels good. I've always felt something missing, and this spirituality fills in a lot of blanks. Believe me, I'm certainly not an angel, and I'm not standing in the streets shouting my religious beliefs. But, it has answered a lot of questions."

Happy but shocked about Eyes's spiritual discovery, Craze thought, "All these years with Eyes, and I never thought once about asking him to attend church or even talk about the subject.

We've literally talked about everything else in the world. How did Peter and I miss that one? For a time, we both practically lived at church, and not once did we invite Eyes—or Lawder for that matter—to join us. I know that I personally questioned the whole 'organized religion' thing during that part of my life, but that's no excuse. How could we be so close to these guys and not share such an important part of our lives? I'm embarrassed."

"Eyes's 50th"

In his younger days, Eyes always told Craze, "I'm retiring when I'm forty five so I have plenty of time to do the things I want to do in my life."

On Eyes's fiftieth birthday, Craze called Eyes and mockingly asked, "Hey man, you always said you were retiring at forty five, it's five years later. What's the deal?"

After a few moments of silence, Eyes slowly responded, "Well Craze It's like this...these guys keep sending me these huge checks every week. It's smart on their part to pay me weekly, because it's a constant reminder of why I keep going to work. As long as these checks keep coming in, I guess I'll keep accepting them."

ON TO PETER'S FILE
"Peter Back on Track"

Ironically, after Eyes's first year of college, Peter enrolled at the same local art college. Peter, a year younger than Eyes, and who, along with Craze, had dreamed up the band many years ago while melting crayons on a church radiator, KNEW what his future held. He focused like a laser on his original passion, his spiritual conviction and classical piano. Peter traveled as far as

Paris with a seemingly unquenchable thirst for seeking a higher level of knowledge in classical piano and how it affected religion. Faith guided his voyage. Craze pulled a letter from the drawer:

> During *The Public Service* years, I ignored classical piano and devoted all my attention to you guys and rock music. I wouldn't give up that time for anything, but there was no doubt in my mind where my future lay. Ever since the sixth grade when me and my 'girlfriend' heard my first classical piano piece on the radio, I knew my pathway in life."

Craze remembered, "like it was yesterday," that day long ago in Sunday school when Peter announced with confidence, "I'm gonna be a classical pianist." After Peter's announcement Craze thought, "It seemed like only a week or two went by before Peter was playing classical music on the church piano; and boy, was he good at it."

"Organ-Boy Peter"

After the break-up of the band, and thinking his rock music days were over, Peter got a call from Billy (Mr. Tick, tick, tick). "Hey man, last night after rehearsal, my manager told me to bring *"organ-boy* from your old band" to the next practice. Obviously he meant you. How about it, you interested?"

Peter answered, "How much? Does the gig pay well? Sounds like easy money to me. What do you think?"

"Yeah, well the music is a piece of cake. We don't do anything as complicated as our old band. The only thing is that the manager is a pain in the butt. He controls everything; so don't plan on getting creative with the tunes. It's more like having a job than playing in a band; that part took a little getting used to at first."

"Well, I guess it pays a lot more than working at *Sears* and getting paid minimum wage, so count me in."

After a short stint with the band, Peter's interest in rock music quickly faded, and his fervor for his first loves, classical music and religion, took over. He did experiment on a couple of rock recording projects with Billy and Lawder. But for Peter, the writing "was on the wall." He totally immersed himself in studying, piano, religion, and teaching. As in his baptism much earlier in his life, Peter directed his entire being into the world of religion and its effects on classical music.

"Peter returns to the scene of the crime"

Long after his days at *Webster College*, Peter called Craze.

"Craze, you won't believe this. I just played a concert at *Eden Seminary* sponsored by *Webster College* and *Eden*; a *Mozart* program called, 'Mozart and Mulled Cider.' We played all authentic 18th century replica instruments—fortepiano, violin, and cello—no less. And guess what? It took place in THE SAME HALL that we played OUR first gig, and all I could think about was *The Public Service's* grand finale. We played 'Wild Thing' for FORTY-FIVE MINUTES!! I continued my *Mozart*, but I couldn't wipe the *Public Service* smile off my face.

"Peter Piled High and Deep"

Comfortably settled in Columbia by this time, Craze answered the phone. On the other end, Peter said, "Hey man, I'm back."

"Man, it's great to hear your voice. 'Long time no see.' I've been dying to hear about your trip; tell me all about it." Craze started taking notes for the drawer.

"Man there's so much to tell. Let me put it this way: I've learned so much; I've been 'lock-smiting with 88 keys' across Europe for the last 12 months, studying for my degree. I spent most of my time in Paris and did some research in Poland studying the relationships between classical music and religion—right up my alley. I also continued studying classical piano and guess what? I've been accepted into the Julliard Ph.D. program in piano performance. I'm gonna call it a 'Piled High and Deep' degree. You better start practicing calling me 'Doctor Peter' in a couple of years."

Proud of his lifelong friend, Craze answered, "Yeah, well I'll promise you this much, I might practice calling you Doctor...or maybe something else...but you might not like my choice."

"Dog Food Commercial"

After achieving his PhD, Peter joined forces with Eyes on two projects: a huge classical project, recording a full production of *Handel's* Messiah...and a dog food commercial.

Craze asked, "So how did that work out; which one paid the most?"

The now "Doctor Peter" answered, "Man, it's no contest; the dog food commercial paid really well. On the other hand, the *Messiah* album's been out for a few years as a Christmas record and I still haven't made a dime. But it sure was fun to make."

"Peter and The Pictures"

Craze's mind wandered back to a conversation that he and Peter had had many years earlier. While looking through an old trunk, Craze had discovered a pile of individual photos of each member of the band from back in the day. Craze knew how rare the photos were because the band rarely ever had their pictures taken. Craze pored over the pictures, kept a few photos, and then passed the rest around to the other guys, offering each to take what pictures they wanted.

After the pictures were dispersed and the remaining ones sent back to Craze, he and Peter talked on the phone. By now, they both had growing kids and Craze innocently asked Peter, "Well what did your kids think about the pictures?"

Craze waited for a funny response, but Peter's answer shocked Craze. "Oh, well I didn't show them to anybody. I don't want them to know I had long hair."

For years after, a thought had smoldered in the back of Craze's mind, "Maybe Peter's embarrassed by us and what we stood for."

Over those years, Craze even discussed the statement with Eyes and Lawder. Lawder had responded, "Well Craze, you, more than any of us, know how he feels about religion. Maybe you're right. Maybe he is embarrassed. But I know by his responses when we talk that he still has respect for us."

And Eyes said, "It's entirely possible that he is embarrassed, I just don't really know how to take it. But don't you ever forget, he'll always be one of US."

Years had passed when Craze finally got up the guts to bring up the old comment. He asked, "Peter, remember the time I sent you those pictures, and you said that you didn't show them to your kids? Did the pictures somehow embarrass you or make you feel uncomfortable?"

Peter replied, "Craze let me tell you a story. Believe me, I've never been embarrassed by you guys or what the band accomplished. But I want you to understand where my brain was twenty years ago. Remember, I spent all those years completely devoted to my religious beliefs and classical music. I got so deeply involved that I began to believe that my children shouldn't see me in long hair. I also thought my peers would look down on me for participating in rock music. So I didn't share that part of my life with anybody.

"A few years ago, I got a job as the director of music at this huge church just outside of Chicago. I was proud of the fact that I had won that position over many other people who had applied.

"One day my boss pulled me aside and said, 'I guess you've wondered why you were the guy I hired out of all those other applicants?' I admitted that the thought had crossed my mind more than once. My boss responded, 'The Grateful Dead…that's why I hired you. You had personal experience with *The Grateful Dead* and other icons in the rock business. That separated you apart from all the other applicants. Nobody else had had those kinds of experiences, and I needed somebody comfortable in dealing with major acts. So *The Grateful Dead* is the reason that I hired you.'

"I was dumbfounded by his answer. I must admit, I did feel embarrassed by my long hair and all. I mentioned *The Dead* and all the others in my interview, hoping he'd overlook that part of my life. But it turned out that it actually helped get me the job. That one comment by my boss made me realize that my reservations were unfounded, and I don't feel that way anymore because *The Grateful Dead* got me that job."

When he got off the phone, Craze contacted Lawder and Eyes and filled them in on this new information about their old friend, Peter. Craze jokingly added, "I don't know what all the fuss was about, anyway. Except for shorter hair, and a few wisps of grey, Peter looks like he did forty years ago. And by the way, he also still acts like a dork."

"Peter's Piano"

Peter proudly announced, "Guess what man? I just bought *Brian Wilson* of *The Beach Boys'* grand piano for the church. The piano is already wired for sound and it is cool! For all I know, it might be the same one he wrote all those songs for *Pet Sounds*, when *The Beatles* turned around and broke his heart with *Sgt. Pepper's*."

𝄞

For Peter, the writing was on the wall; he spent his life totally immersing himself in studying, piano, religion, and teaching.

FINALLY, LAWDER'S FILE
"Lawder Also Finds Religion"

Lawder also followed a religious path, but with a COMPLETELY different twist. First he played with a couple local bands, then moved to Champaign, Illinois, and did a short stint with *REO Speedwagon*. After leaving *REO*, Lawder moved back to St Louis and joined forces with former *Ike and Tina Turner* background singer *Marcel Strong*, doing covers from the likes of *Johnny Taylor, Al Green* and *The Temptations*. Lawder officially became part of *Marcel's* hot back-up band...*The Sex Machine*. Eventually Lawder left *The Sex Machine* for more money. The drummer in *Marcel's* band introduced Lawder to *The Right Reverend David Epley* out of Chicago who had now settled at the corner of Locust and Garrison in the inner city of St. Louis and the home of *The Baptist Church of the Good Shepherd*. Lawder had finally returned to his old neighborhood in the inner city. Not lead by faith, but money, Lawder became the permanent bassist for the *Reverend's* Gospel group.

Lawder had no idea that his journey to manhood would include such an eye-opening, wild ride. Along the way, Lawder met the *Reverend Shoutin' Hayes* who testified at every out of town tent revival. Lawder mimicked the Reverend's voice as he quoted his story, "They tied me to the back of a '57 Chevrolet, drug me through the streets and set my leg on fire. I prayed to the lord, 'GET BACK DEVILS'! Then the Lord set me free and healed me...HAIL!"

Lawder described an incident to Craze that happened during a revival in New York City. "My drummer buddy and I got the job of assisting in *The Annual Resurrection of Christ Service*. Get this, each year, an East Indian fellow arrived in New York and volunteered to play the part of Christ. He dressed up in a white silk robe with a parachute harness underneath the robes. Before the service the Indian fellow took his center-stage position, lying down in a white silk-lined casket equipped with a black light so the white silk glowed in the dark. During the service, all lights were dimmed down to darkness, allowing the closed casket to glow in the middle of the stage. The drummer and I hid backstage and out of sight.

"With a boat horn strapped behind his back. *The Reverend* would proclaim, 'Gabriel blew his horn...' 'HONK'...again, 'Gabriel blew his horn a second time,' HONK. On the third 'HONK' of Gabriel's horn, the East Indian threw the casket lid open. *The Reverend* would shout, 'Hallelujah.' Glowing in the darkness, the Indian stood up with his arms extended to the heavens. That was our cue to hoist the little guy into the rapture via a rope attached to a pulley and then hooked to the Indian's harness. Hundreds of screaming worshipers, full of the *Holy Ghost*, would run laps around the *Manhattan Center*. On one particular night, we looked up after the lights came back up and realized that the pulley wasn't placed high enough. So the little Indian's black shoes, white socks, and black slacks dangled below the curtain for everybody to see."

"Oh well, I guess it was a limited rapture moment." Lawder jokingly continued, "But you know, I think that rapture must have worked on me. I went to the lobby of the *Manhattan Center* that night and instantly swore off smoking cigarettes."

Lawder approached the vending machine and noticed that price for cigarettes had been raised to SEVENTY-FIVE cents. He took one look at the price and proclaimed,

"That's it, I quit."

"Disciplined"

Craze pulled the next "Lawder" note out of the drawer, which read, "You know, no offense to all the guys I played with over the years, but I never found another band as disciplined as we were in *The Public Service*."

As time went on, a mellowed Lawder joined his son's band playing the blues in the St. Louis area. Lawder joked to Craze, "Hey man I gotta go. I better practice or my son, the boss, will kick my ass out of his band."

"Remember It's Your Job Dummy"

Frustrated by "always being the one who made the calls," Craze told Lawder, "Well, I did it. I told Eyes that the next nickel is on him. If he wants to hear from me again, it's up to him TO CALL ME. I'm always the one who makes the calls, and it's about time he calls me for a change. So I'm gonna wait, however long it takes, for him to call me next time. Let's see how long that takes!"

Lawder angrily responded, "Who do you think you are? How dare you threaten never to call him again? That's always been your job, and it will always continue being your job as long as we're all still alive. You're the leader, the glue that holds us all together. We depend on you to keep us all in touch, so get off your high horse. You promise me right now that you'll continue calling him, or me, or Peter, for that matter, any time it's necessary. Life's too short for that kind of crap."

Stunned by Lawder's words, Craze meekly answered, "Well okay...sorry...I didn't mean to hurt anybody's feelings. I promise I'll call all of you guys whenever it's necessary."

Craze had never felt so comforted by such harsh words... especially from Lawder.

After attending college, Lawder successfully pursued a career as a manufacturing engineer. He continued playing with *The Road Apples*, a popular local band and other acts. Two of the members of the band had earlier joined a young and upcoming bluegrass star named *Vince Gill*. *The Road Apples* played together for over twenty-five years.

Craze slowly replaced the notes and closed the drawer. The beat, the beat goes on...

𝄞

Craze, Eyes, and their wives entered the old movie theater turned into a nightclub in Columbia. No one spoke because no words could describe this almost sacred moment in their lives. The whole thing started so innocently with a phone call from Cody, Eyes's son.

"Hey Craze, it's Cody. My mom and dad told me to call you and ask if you'd keep an eye on me if I moved to Columbia and went to The University of Missouri?"

Craze responded, "Are you nuts? It gets real cold out here. Why don't you just stay in L.A.?"

"Well, I got it down to a choice between Missouri or Montana."

Craze thought for a second and then said, "Sure I'll keep an eye on you...welcome to Missouri!"

So Cody moved to Missouri. The situation got even better. Soon after arriving in Columbia, Cody—quite the guitar player—joined Craze's son, David, in David's band. One weekend, Eyes and his wife made the trek to Columbia for a Parents Weekend at the University. The kids had a surprise for their parents: a concert put on especially for them.

As the couples entered the auditorium, Craze thought, "What are the odds that our two sons would end up playing together and having the same band experiences that Eyes and I did?"

Filled with anticipation, Craze swore that he felt the earth moving beneath his feet. The kids spotted their parents entering the auditorium from the stage and met them halfway into the old theater. To their parents' surprise, Cody and David were wearing *Public Service* t-shirts in honor of their fathers. Then, they proudly handed Eyes and Craze their own shirts to wear that night.

Craze and his wife stood in the back, as usual, taking in the whole scene, while Eyes and Helen stood right in front of Cody's position on stage. The curtain opened and then...all hell broke loose as the band seemingly went crazy banging on their instruments. Craze saw Eyes storming toward him, "They haven't even started playing, and they've already broken a hundred rules!"

Understanding the situation, Craze replied, "Hang on, it's not their fault. This club does their sound checks just before the show starts, so give 'em a minute."

"Well okay, but sound checks just before the show? That's ridiculous!"

After the sound check, the curtain closed, and from the back of the room, Craze noticed Eyes's shoulders relax as the silence returned. Then BANG, the curtains opened with the band tearing the house down with a great original song.

"Hey," Craze thought, "there are at least two more musicians on stage..."

In the almost dark room, Craze also noticed two older guys coming out of doors on the side of the stage, walking straight towards him.

"My eyes are playing tricks on me. That looks like Peter and Lawder. Oh my God... IT IS!"

Craze instantly realized that the two extras on stage were John, Peter's son, and Matt, Lawder's son, also musicians and also wearing *Public Service* shirts. As Peter and Lawder approached Craze, Eyes, who also spotted them, headed for the gathering. Peter shouted over the music, "You can thank your kids for this!"

After the first song and lots of hugs, Lawder spoke up, "Well, we got you guys, didn't we?"

As the guys watched the torch being passed on to their sons, the four guys settled back and listened. David, Craze's son, stepped up to the mic and announced, "This one's for our dads."

David stepped back and counted "one, two, three, four." The sons' band broke into *The Public Service's* former signature song, *The Who's* "My Generation." The old tune brought memories of long ago flowing back into their fathers' minds.

Lawder said, "You know what? If we told other people about everything that's happened to us over the years, they'd call us liars."

Craze thought, "Who's gonna argue with the Volcano…not me."

Still, the beat goes on…

"SEE YOU IN THE AFTERGLOW"

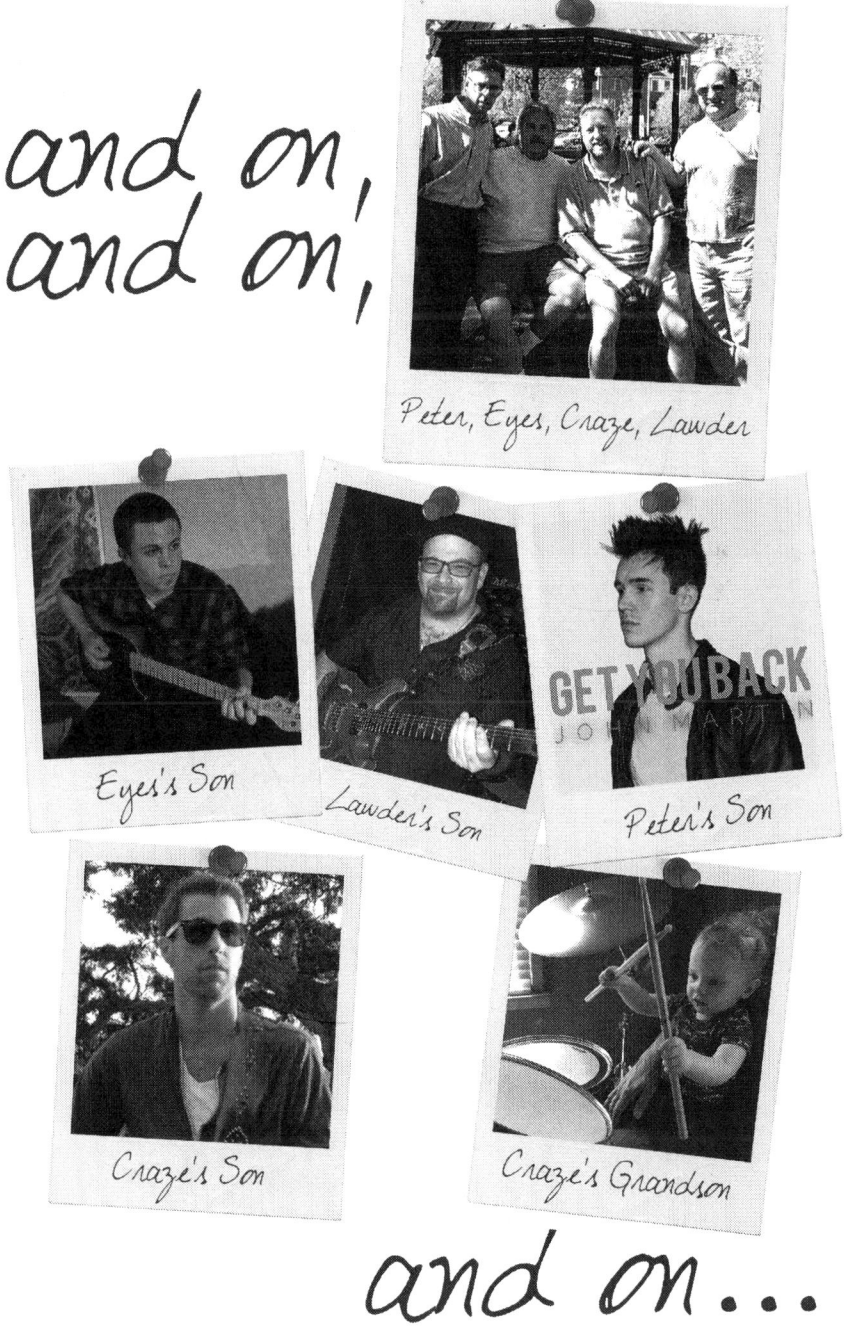

Figure 18. The sons . . . and grandson. Designed by David Kemper, *Cloud Craft Studios*.

Figure 19. Eyes's picture courtesy of Betsey Breckinridge, Lawder, Craze, and Bird pictures courtesy of Bill Mellick, Peter and Billy pictures courtesy of Sandy Ostertag.

A BIBLE FOR BANDS
THE RULES FOR BECOMING A PROFESSIONAL BAND
THE MUSICIAN

1. **You can play in a band**. You must possess: RHYTHM, ENTHUSIASM, GOOD TASTE and the ability to FOLLOW DIRECTIONS.
2. **PRACTICE** your instrument and learn from your mistakes.
3. Put your **soul** into your playing.
4. **Secondary instruments** are fine, but remember which one is truly your **"God given Talent"**.
5. **PLAY IN TUNE**. If you play flat, you can't play. If you sing flat, fix it or don't sing.
6. **Learn your individual part** before rehearsals. Rehearsals are for the group as a whole.
7. **Don't allow distractions**, especially girlfriends (boyfriends), to get in the way.

REHEARSING SONGS

1. **ALL INSTRUMENTS** should follow one of three parts: The rhythm, the hook or the bass line.
2. **Plan your rehearsals** in advance so you don't waste rehearsal time.
3. **Rehearse a song until you're sick of it**, then add the most important part, your soul.
4. **ADD depth to each song** using several different ingredients:
    A. **BEGININGS AND ENDINGS** of a song: **BEGINNINGS** should draw attention to the song. **ENDINGS** should say, **"Don't ever forget me."**
    B. **DYNAMICS**: playing a song at one volume is boring. Give a song life by raising and lowering the volume.

- C. **BREAKS**: draw attention to parts of the song with silence. The sudden silence draws attention to the song.
- D. **HOOKS** are the parts of the music that everybody "hums". Besides the words, it's what everybody remembers about the song.
- E. **UNCONVENTIONAL CHORD CHANGES** make the song go somewhere totally unexpected.
- F. **LEADS can include more than one instrument**, which will accent the IT even more.

5. Don't arbitrarily **change your part on stage**.
6. **Too many TECHNIQUES** in one song can lead to a jumbled mess.
7. **Focus your attention on one person** in the audience and observe their reaction to the show.

THE BAND

1. **Keep a little of that dirt** from the garage **in your music**.
2. **Your band is a machine and you're a cog**. The machine only works when each part is synced with the others.
3. Playing in a **band is a business**: the more people buying your product, the more successful the band.
4. Playing in a **band is an art**. So use your imagination and **think out of the box** sometimes.
5. **Star quality** and **arrogance** differ as do **confidence and cocky**.
6. **Overinflated egos** have no place on a team and are the **most destructive force in a band**.
7. If any **member starts blaming the listener**; it might be **time for them to leave**.
8. **Great musicians don't necessarily know how to run a band.** Find out who is the best leader.
9. **Discuss problems** otherwise they will only grow.

THE SHOW

1. The show actually begins before you go on stage, so **look the part**. Your **stage presence** must be genuine, natural, and confident.
3. Leave your **bad mood** behind. Nobody wants to see a grump. It's a show, so act!
4. **Adjust your sound to fit the room**. Rooms vary from booming gyms to acoustically perfect auditoriums.
5. The same principals in constructing a song are used in designing your show; they both have a **beginning, middle and end**.
    A. **THE BEGINING** of a show is the "attention getter", so start out with a bang. Nothing should be heard from the stage until the first note of the first song. Use your second best song. Some examples:
        — The entire band enters together, picks up their instruments, and starts the first song.
        — **Don't** mosey on stage or start tuning or goof around.
        — Play an intro-song and then make a big deal out of your front person's entry.
        — Say, "Wake up, "We've arrived and we're going to blow your minds".
        — Once you have the crowd's attention, **never lose it**.
    B. **THE MIDDLE** of the show should say, **"I'm taking you on a journey and keeping you entertained without interruption."** Design your sets to ebb and flow dynamically mixing both fast and slow songs.

    Plan what happens between songs and do not allow "Dead silence". Use these breaks as weapons, not distractions. Announce upcoming shows or introduce the next song. A good story always works. Never play your instrument between songs.

Make the audience think that, **"This is the place I want to be."** Suggestion: Play songs in rapid-fire succession with no breaks at all.

C. **The END OF EACH SET** and **especially THE END OF THE SHOW should be spectacular**. Save your best song for last. Give them something that they will remember and make them want to see you again. Then, get off the stage; **the show is over**.

Don't let your excitement destroy the finale by screaming in the mic, banging on the drums or going nuts on the guitar.

NOW, finish your job; go out in the crowd and talk to your fans.

6. **Sell yourself on and off stage**. Hang out with the audience during breaks and treat them with respect. They will remember how you treated them.

7. **The stage is the worst place to balance sound**: Find out what it sounds like from the audience's perspective. The best solution is to have your own soundman.

8. **Don't apologize** for mistakes; it just draws more attention to the slip-up.

9. **Speak clearly** and annunciate when speaking into a microphone.

10. **Don't upstage** the lead by **"stepping on"** or **drowning out** a solo.

11. **The lead should dominate**, then, fall back into line with the others.

12. **If you cannot hear yourself**, solve the problem.

13. **Communicate**: There are two types: **ON STAGE communication** between band members and **ON STAGE TO OFF STAGE communication** between back stage, the sound Booth, and equipment managers.

14. **The show should be seamless** so that it continually entertains the audience.

15. **The show is all about your fans** so, make them want to come back again and bring their friends.

SONGWRITERS

1. **Songwriters write songs to inspire people** and they must share that emotion with the world. A great song is a great concept that others understand.

2. **Good songwriters are bursting with many ideas**. If one idea doesn't work, they have plenty more.

3. **Many songwriters cannot be impartial judges** of their own songs; the songs are pieces of their souls. So by it's very nature, they are the worst judges of their own music.

4. **Smart writers invite constructive criticism.**

5. **Most songs aren't hits.**

6. Musicians:

    A. **be careful how you handle negative responses to a songwriter's song** or you might lose a writer.

    B. If a writer insists on **playing an inferior song**, just play the song; there's too much at stake, like the coherence of the band.

    C. Using the **audience's response** is the **safest way to reason with a writer** about a badly written song.

7. Don't let learning how to write songs **"the right way"** pollute your creativity.

8. **Play your song with** as much **emotion** as it took to write it.